D0908889

[EASTERN]

THE CIVILIZED BODY

THE CIVILIZED BODY

Social Domination, Control, and Health

Peter E. S. Freund
with the assistance of
Miriam Fisher

Temple University Press
PHILADELPHIA

Temple University Press
© 1982 by Temple University. All rights reserved
Published 1982
Printed in the United States of America

Library of Congress Cataloging in Publication Data

Freund, Peter E. S.
    The civilized body.

    Includes bibliographical references and index.
    1. Social medicine.   2. Power (Social sciences)   3. Mind and
body.   I. Fisher, Miriam.   II. Title.
RA418.F75 1982   362.1'042   82-10787
ISBN 0-87722-285-1

The Sweatshop

I   The machines in the shop, so wildly they roar
That oft I forget in their roar that I am.
In the terrible tumult I'm buried
The me is all gone, a machine, I become
I work, work, work on unceasing;
'Tis toil, toil, toil unending.
Why? For whom? I know not, I ask not.
A machine? How can it e'er fashion a thought?

II   No room for feelings, for thought or for reason,
All bitter and bloody the work kills the noblest,
The best, the most beautiful, the richest, the deepest.
The highest in life is crushed to the earth
On fly the seconds, the minutes, the hours,
The nights like the days flee swiftly as sails;
I drive the machine as though I would catch them,
Unavailing I chase them, unceasing I speed.

III   The clock in the workshop is never at rest;
Ever pointing and ticking and waking together.
Its ticking and waking had meaning, they told me.
And reason was in it, they said to me then;
And still something as though a dream, I remember;
Life sense and the something the clock wakens in me—
What it is, I forget; ask me now!
I know not, I know not, I am a machine!

IV   And then, at times, the clock I hear,
Its pointing, its language, I understand different;
Its unrest (pendulum) pushes me onward.
"Work more, more, much more"
In its sound the angry words of the boss,
In its two hands his gloomy face I see.
The clock, I shudder—it seems to drive and cry!
"Machine," and shriek out, "sew, sew."

A Yiddish Song by Morris Rosenfeld, *Coast Seamen's Journal*, June 22, 1898; cited from *American Labor Songs of the Nineteenth Century* (Urbana, Illinois: University of Illinois Press, 1975).

Contents

Acknowledgments

Without the help of my friends, this project would not have come to fruition. Miriam Fisher, M. S., patiently worked with me, clarifying my ideas and written style. She infused the work with vitality and gave me the encouragement I needed. Her talents in communicating ideas, analyzing them, and her good solid common sense were indispensable to this work. Dr. Ralph Larkin's penetrating critical comments and close reading of the manuscript were invaluable. Dr. Mona Abrams, with her ability to think clearly, offered perceptive criticisms and editorial assistance. Further thanks for reading this work are due to Dr. Meredith McGuire, Dr. George Martin and Dr. Barbara Chasin (all of them my colleagues at Montclair State College). My students at Montclair State College were constant sources of energy. My thanks to the editors and staff at Temple University Press, especially for the supportive help of Michael Ames and for Michael Fisher's keen eye. Ms. Lisa Isenstead helped me with the typing of drafts and her honest observations. Ms. Dolores Henricksen typed the final draft with great precision and craftsmanship. Finally, my thanks must go to Igor Freund whose ability to retrieve materials was most helpful.

Preface

During the past ten years, I've had a chance to observe, in the chronic back problem of my closest friend, the subtle interplay between an individual's social power, the way that person responds to powerlessness, and the career of his/her illness, as well as the intensity of symptoms. This experience led to my interest in teaching a course on the sociology of health and illness. Through preparing this course and dialogues with my students, I was not only helped in clarifying my thoughts and reactions, but provided with an opportunity to investigate the manifold ways in which societies can affect health. The interpenetration of society and the body is a most fascinating one.

In reviewing the literature, I was struck by the timidity of sociologists in exploring such a topic. They, generally speaking, uncritically accepted the orthodox medical view of human beings, and almost seemed in awe of what they perceived as Medical Terrain. Most of my research thus led me to "psychological" and holistic medicine. My interest in holistic medicine had also been sparked by my friend's search for alternatives in light of the failure of what even the best of modern allopathic medicine (complete with microsurgery) offered. Traditional doctors did not seem particularly receptive to other "unspectacular" forms of treatment such as massage. In the holistic approach, I found a different, more comprehensive, dynamic notion of health than found among doctors who treated my friend's body as a machine upon which they could display their technical virtuosity.

My background in radical sociology and affinity to "neo-Marxism," with their healthy emphasis on power and "economic" factors, provided me lenses with which to view not only these personally related experiences, but to address the more general question of the relationship of society to health. I found the attempts in radical, neo-Marxist writings to formulate general theories about how social arrangements can make one sick to be a promising beginning. I hope I can aid their development.

The reader will note the absence (with one or two exceptions) of any references to mental health. Though much of what will be discussed about the social sources of physical illness might also be applied to "madness," or "neurosis," I have avoided making the assumption that psychic conflicts can be viewed as illnesses. It is questionable whether or not what much of what is labeled madness is really a medical problem. More likely, mental illness is the residual, catch-all category for all of those behaviors that cannot be readily understood. Extreme nonconformity, disruptive responses to severe stress, and mood changes due to biochemical factors are all subsumed under the same category—mental illness. The label has frequently been indiscriminately applied, and at times for "political" reasons. Thus unmanageable rebellion against repressive parents, for instance, may result in a "diagnosis" applied by psychiatric specialists acting in collusion with parental authority. Such a label not only makes the individual's response seem "irrational" but can mystify a repressive, unnurturing family existence.

Aside from my objections to viewing most mental illness as a "real" medical entity, I have also found that, when sociologists wish to demonstrate the interplay between society and illness, they mainly gravitate to such "fuzzy" types of illnesses. I don't find the idea that so-called "mental health" is affected by the social environment half as intriguing as the idea that social arrangements have clear *somatic* consequences. I prefer to limit myself to those illnesses that medical expertise can identify with greater precision and those problems on which there is relative consensus that there is a manifestly physiological component. While mental illness is well worth analyzing as a "socially constructed" reality, I don't wish to take the position or even imply that it has a physical basis.

Even though the title of my work promises to discuss civilization, I certainly do not mean to equate this country with Western civilization. While not all my examples and sources are from the United States, the focus is, in fact, primarily on this country—particularly because American-based researchers, sociologists, and others are doing most of the work in this area. Furthermore, it is in this country that the socio-cultural contradictions of monopoly capitalism appear to be most clearly discernible.

My emphasis in this book is not only on those large-scale mechanisms of social control that are a general part of the social order but also on specific institutional ones (for example, work settings). Society, among other things, is a complex matrix of institutional structures interspersed with lacunae of uninstitutionalized social worlds. My work emphasizes how the techniques and effects of social control in one institutional sphere can be diffused into other institutional spheres (e.g., schools inculcate factory and work discipline and prepare students for work).

Before I embark on my project, a word about words is in order. My references to "the body" may appear laden with mechanical metaphors in many places. I speak of "yoking the body," for instance. The intention behind such a usage is twofold. First of all, I use these various metaphors to emphasize the systemic nature of the body and its processes; secondly, such terms more effectively highlight the oppressive and somatic effects that social "forces" can have on our bodies. It should be kept in mind that these are metaphors, not literal descriptions.

I have discovered that the most exciting areas are those that transcend disciplinary confines, and thus, even though I am a sociologist, speak a sociologist's language, and my purpose is to contribute to that discipline, I hope that those interested in health, political activists, psychologists, and many others will enjoy and benefit from their encounter with this work. I will now begin to explore the interesting interplay between our social arrangements and our physical well-being.

THE CIVILIZED BODY

CHAPTER ONE

Introduction: Social Control and Health

THE SOCIAL CONTEXTS OF HEALTH

As there are many ways to live, there are also many ways to get sick and die. Human beings share with other living creatures on this earth a vulnerability to myriad sources of disease, to wear and tear, and to total breakdown. What distinguishes us from other species is our creativity in inventing new ways of making ourselves sick, maiming, and killing each other. Much of this self-destruction develops from the ways in which men and women collectively engage in material production, cultural activities, the raising of children, play, and so forth. Work can make us sick and so can being a parent or child. As Eric Eckholm (1977) has so cogently put it—each society, in producing its own way of life, produces its own way of death. Of course, these ways change over time due to the manner in which we structure and style our lives and due to the effects such different social-economic forces have on us.

In the West, recent changes in the material, physical, and social environment have had an effect on the nature of health problems. Dubos (1968A: 54) describes some of these changes. In most parts of the world, "natural" forces such as famine still rule.

> More and more, however, man is now responsible for the introduction of new environmental factors that condition and often threaten all aspects of his life. During the early phases of the Industrial Revolution, infectious processes, nutritional deficiencies, hard physical labor, and the sudden migration from sparsely populated areas to congested and unsanitary urban environments were among the factors that affected the proletariat most severely. The bourgeois classes had their own problems, originating from overeating, lack of physical exercise, and other misuse of economic affluence, as well as from the psychological constraints created by unreasonable social conventions. In our own societies, the influences of material wealth and of the industrial environment are now compounded by the effects of generalized urbanization.

For most of the population in Western society "absolute" material scarcity has all but disappeared. The tremendous material surplus generated by modern capitalism has led some to describe American society, beginning around the 1950s, as a "post-scarcity society"[1] (Bookchin, 1971). With the lessening of material scarcity, malnutrition and the attendant susceptibility to infectious diseases have declined. Furthermore, most infectious diseases themselves (except perhaps for sexually transmitted ones) have been brought under control through public health measures that began in the late 19th century (Berliner and Salmon, 1979).

Many of us are now "victims" of what Eckholm (1977) calls the affluent diet. Obesity, aggravated by a sedentary life

---

[1]We should remember that there are still pockets of malnutrition and starvation even in countries such as the United States. Moreover, much of America's material surplus is a product of worldwide imperialist resource-hogging rather than merely technological development. Nor should we forget that the notion of "post-scarcity" does not apply to most of the world, and thus many of the problems raised in this essay are not a high priority for much of humankind. The first item on the agenda for them should be a form of socialism that provides for fundamental material needs.

style, has become a new and prominent health problem.[2] The nature of the foods we eat has changed in recent generations. Our diet is relatively protein-rich and in many ways nutritious. Yet it is also filled with chemical additives that increasingly are being discovered to be carcinogenic. Foods are highly processed, and this processing may be linked to such problems as digestive disorders. Such foods may also be lacking in equivalent nutrition compared with unprocessed foods.

Though many of the physical and biochemical stressors of the past have been brought under control, new dangers arise from what Bookchin (1962) calls our "synthetic" environment. Our air and water are increasingly polluted. New "human-made" pollutants (for instance, the plastic products of the petrochemical industry, not found in nature) permeate our surroundings.[3] Our ability to produce new chemicals outstrips our ability to predict their full consequences. While many new chemicals are introduced annually into manufacturing, only a few have been tested for their long-range effects on health (Stellman and Daum, 1971). Auto emissions, ranging from sulfur dioxide to lead particulates, contribute, it has been estimated, to about one-half of urban pollution (DeBell, 1970). The production process that makes autos, plastics, pesticides and other products of progress burns large amounts

[2]Of course, for the lower classes, obesity may be caused by high-starch diets.

[3]The phrase, "human-made" pollutants, is deceptive since the technologies and industries that are the greatest polluters are controlled, encouraged, and abused by the corporate sector. As Bookchin (1962: lix) points out, the "we" in such phrases as "we pollute" is a gloss that equates the urban litterer with the Hooker Chemical Company (of Niagara Falls notoriety). Nor are "we" all equally exposed to pollution. People who produce, work, or, by virtue of their work, are forced to live near pollutants become human guinea pigs who encounter pollutants in a more concentrated form. Despite claims that urban executives breathe the same smog as workers, the hidden price of "progress" may be greater for some than others. The tendency to gloss over the relationship between power and exposure to health hazards, in this case, pollution, also manifests itself when "we" talk about other "stressors," such as social-psychological ones. This will be explored later.

of coal and other natural fuels. Radiation, not only from nuclear power but from other sources such as microwaves, adds to this attack. All these forces in turn contribute to assaults on the environment and the individuals who live in it.

Changing environmental and social conditions are reflected, as I mentioned earlier, in changing health problems. In most of the Western world, infectious diseases have declined since the early part of the twentieth century (McKeown, 1979) and chronic diseases such as ulcers, coronary heart disease, diabetes, arthritis and cancer have increased (Doyal, 1981: 59). The increased incidence of these diseases cannot be attributed simply, as has been argued, to twentieth-century advances in longevity because, beginning in the 1950s, even *younger* age groups have shown an increased incidence of these afflictions. (Eyer and Sterling, 1977; Bellingall, 1979). The premature wearing down of the body is thus apparent, and may be the result not only of new dietary and environmental factors, but of social factors as well. Evidence that the social, biochemical and physical environment of industrialized societies generate new health problems (such as increased rates of cancer) comes from a comparison with "pre-industrial" societies, which have lower incidence of these problems. Again, increased lifespan in Western countries does not fully account for the variations, since the rates of "diseases of civilization" increase among groups that move from agricultural to industrial communities (Doyal, 1981; Powles, 1973).[4] Though Antonovsky (1979: 193) argues that when a certain standard of living is reached psychosocial influences replace biochemical and physical stressors as the main determinants of health, what

[4]These observations should not be taken to mean that I believe "pre-industrial" societies were free of biochemical-physical stressors, much less psychosocial ones. Interpersonal violence was a significant source of stress in medieval European society, for instance, despite a presumably higher tolerance for violence among its members (Elias, 1978). On the whole, people did not live long enough to die from stress.

has just been said about modern synthetic environments forces us to qualify his observation and to take into account additional factors. Still, there is no doubt that the prosperity generated by modern capitalism (along with the sanitary, welfare and public health measures capitalist societies have been forced to adopt) has changed the nature of health problems (particularly for the upper and middle classes). These changes warrant a strong emphasis on the role of psychosocial factors.

BODILY REGULATION

Research in psychological medicine has begun to establish endocrinological and other physiological bridges between social pressures and disease. Hans Selye's pioneering work on stress (1956) has been followed by other investigators, who have focused on the way in which responses to stress affect health. For instance, Benson (1979) studied the importance of relaxation in dealing with stress; and Friedman and Rosenman (1974) have suggested that there may be a coronary-disease-prone pattern of behavior (a personal style they call "Type A," which is competitive, hostile, obsessed with time and self-control). Over and over again, research has demonstrated the importance to health of mind-body integration, equilibrium in bodily functions and the ability of the body to follow its own rhythm. For instance, the ability to mobilize the body, to muster its defenses, seems to involve the desire of the organism to go on living. The "will to live" is a metaphor for the motive force that energizes the body and strengthens its defenses. Norman Cousins (1976), in his bout with life-threatening illness, found that only by "resettling"—taking responsibility for—his body could he mobilize its healing resources. He experienced the will to live as having a physiological basis and, in many respects, engineered his own cure. Schmale (1972) speculates that perhaps "giving up" on a psychological level has its biological counterpart on a cellular level. Speculative as this observation is, it is nonetheless possible that a loss of existential purpose and surrender of the reins of control over one's body may set into motion certain adverse physiological processes.

I shall refer to these factors that play an important part in health as forms of "bodily regulation" and those that play a part in illness as "bodily deregulation."[5] Bodily regulation is possible only if the body has a reasonable amount of control over its external environment. The world outside the body, for instance, must move at a pace that is in tune with the body's capabilities; it must be, to some degree, predictable, intelligible, etc. The body must also be able to regulate its internal environment. It must be able to recognize and monitor information about itself (e.g., pain), and be able to mobilize and defend itself against environmental stressors. As a part of being in touch with itself, the body must allow the operation of "automatic" regulating forces, such as the "relaxation response"—the body's ability to relax (Benson, 1979).

Thus, to be in control over one's inner environment requires not only voluntary control but the ability to bring into play the body's automatic regulating forces. Bodily regulation is therefore not synonymous with conscious self-control.[6] From this viewpoint, "letting go" is a form of bodily

---

[5]Bakan's (1968) concept of "telic decentralization" is very close to my own notion of "bodily deregulation." Disease involves a "degree of telic decentralization," and pain is the psychological expression of such "decentralization." Such "decentralization" is the result of a communication breakdown between various parts of the body that can occur on many levels, including the cellular. More recently, Schwartz (1979) has used the term "disregulation" essentially the way I do. Though he stresses that "disregulation" can occur on atomic, chemical, biological or social levels, his focus is, in fact, on the central nervous system. Like myself, he finds "disregulation" a useful concept since it allows for consideration of "a range of different mechanisms whereby disconnections between people and the environment as well as between various systems within people themselves can contribute to disorder and disease" (564).

[6]One need not even be subjectively aware of a lack of bodily regulation, since the consequences of its absence often will manifest themselves only when clinically observable signs appear and the body breaks down in signifi-

regulation that allows the musculature to relax, certain responses such as orgasm to occur spontaneously and permits information from the body's external and internal environment to be "heard." Paradoxically, not being able to relinquish control can often result in a loss of "control" over the body. Therefore "regulation" is a more appropriate and descriptive term than control. As Pelletier suggests, regulation can be defined as "harmonious integration of voluntary and autonomic processes" (1977: 26–27). For bodily "regulation" the mind actively collaborates with physiological processes. The true meaning of "psychosomatic" here then is not the simplistic idea of control by the mind "over" the body, but is rather an interactive process, psyche and soma influencing each other.

What appears to be a metaphorical use of the term bodily regulation has a physiological basis that is supported by the literature of holistic and psychological medicine. A loss of bodily regulation in its physiological forms, for instance, may involve throwing the nervous system and/or endocrinological systems "out of kilter" with attendant effects on the working state of particular organs, and on the body's defense system and its informational feedback. This essay will link the ability of the person to consciously as well as "automatically" manage the functioning of his or her mind-body system to social factors.

A review of the literature makes it clear that power is one such significant social factor affecting health, and I will focus on one way in which power is used in societies—for social control. The contemporary forms of powerlessness, such as a "harried lifestyle," are usually seen as one of the effects of civilization. But they are, as I will soon spell out, the result of highly developed, entrenched forms of control that support the hierarchical relationships in "modern" and "civilized"

---

cant ways. Bodily awareness, also is socially mediated and systems of domination affect such awareness by discouraging or encouraging attention to various parts of the body and bodily signals. (For a very readable account of some of the factors that affect body awareness, see Fisher, 1973.)

societies. Before I elaborate on this specific relationship between civilized social control, social domination and the
ability of the body-mind system to efficiently and effectively
manage its internal affairs, a brief discussion of the more
general relationship between power and health is necessary.

POWER AND HEALTH

Power is a central resource of social life. Its distribution
affects not only our access to the material and social resources that allow for survival but also our very ability to
live, in a *qualitative* sense, a healthy and long life. Power is
linked to both social and physical life chances. Our social
power, for instance, is an important contingency in allowing
us to obtain high quality, readily available medical care, and,
of course, it affects the degree to which we can exercise
control of our care (Waitzkin and Waterman, 1974). How
much power we have, how we use it to regulate our lives, and
how much power we *subjectively* feel we have can also affect
us physiologically. In his animal experiments and review of
the literature, Seligman (1975) has shown the relationship to
health of both "giving up" and powerlessness. Schmale
(1972) also has shown that "giving up" can be a significant
catalyst of disease. Powerlessness can, in itself, make one
sick, as the following incident illustrates.

> This writer witnessed one such case of death due to a loss of
> will within a psychiatric hospital. A female patient who had
> remained in a mute state for nearly 10 years was shifted to a
> different floor of her building along with her floor mates, while
> her unit was being redecorated. The third floor of this
> psychiatric unit where the patient in question had been living
> was known among the patients as the chronic, hopeless floor.
> In contrast, the first floor was most commonly occupied by
> patients who held privileges, including the freedom to come
> and go on the hospital grounds and to the surrounding streets.
> In short, the first floor was an exit ward from which patients

could anticipate discharge fairly rapidly. All patients who were temporarily moved from the third floor were given medical examinations prior to the move, and the patient in question was judged to be in excellent medical health though still mute and withdrawn. Shortly after moving to the first floor, this chronic psychiatric patient surprised the ward staff by becoming socially responsive such that within a two-week period she ceased being mute and was actually becoming gregarious. As fate would have it, the redecoration of the third-floor unit was soon completed and all previous residents were returned to it. Within a week after she had been returned to the "hopeless" unit, this patient, who like the legendary Snow White had been aroused from a living torpor, collapsed and died. The subsequent autopsy revealed no pathology of note, and it was whimsically suggested at the time that the patient had died of despair. (Lefcourt, 1973: 422)

A sociologist writing the death certificate might have noted "death by institutional invalidation" as the cause. The conditions of powerlessness that led her to despair were a normal, built-in consequence of her social role as an inmate of what Goffman (1961) calls a "total institution."[7] The stratification system of the total institution, with its extremely asymmetrical power relationships, "short circuits" the flow of information between the inmate and those who run the asylum. These are the kinds of debilitating social circumstances that will be examined in this essay.

One's social class position is another rough expression of the amount of social power one possesses. Social class is determined individually by income, occupation, education, or a combination of these dimensions. Generally speaking, the higher one's social status, the less vulnerable one is to illness and disease. Studies have repeatedly shown, for in-

---

[7]In *Asylums* Goffman defines total institutions as hybrids between communities and formal bureaucratic organizations. In such places as monasteries, prisons, and mental hospitals, usually isolated from the civilian world, every facet of the inmate's life is planned, managed and surveyed by the staff, which has a great social and psychological distance from the inmate's world.

stance, a relationship between social class and illness. These differences in health between social classes have, furthermore, persisted since about 1900 (Syme and Berkman, 1976). Yet to focus simply on the life circumstances of those who possess the least social power would lead one to ignore a number of significant ways in which power relationships can have sickening consequences for those who, in fact, appear to have a great deal of social power. While the upper classes are favored on all measures of life expectancy and contract fewer infectious diseases, heart disease is more prevalent among them. Cervical cancer is more prevalent in the lower class, but breast cancer is more of an upper-class malady (Cockerham, 1978: 40). Thus, while the *general* relationship between class and health holds, certain diseases are more common to the upper classes. Most significantly, while elderly, poor, black and other minorities have higher morbidity rates, these differences do not explain morbidity or mortality rates and patterns within the general population. As Antonovsky argues, "the salutogenic (health-generating) question is hardly less pertinent to white middle-class and non-elderly people than it is to those more discriminated against" (1979: 35).

Eyer's (1975) study of the sources of hypertension in modern societies, as well as his work with Sterling on stressors endemic to capitalistic social organization (Eyer and Sterling, 1977), are significant examples of attempts to systematically link health to structurally generated powerlessness. In his work on hypertension, he reviews some of the usual correlates of high blood pressure (high-fat diet, lack of exercise, and others) and concludes that the most significant cause of hypertension is the loss of certain crucial forms of control produced by modern class structures. For instance, such societies demand time-pressured work and create other forms of economic-social powerlessness. In a later work (Eyer and Sterling, 1977), he and Sterling move beyond the bounds of this one complex of "symptoms" (i.e., hypertension) by using the concept of stress.[8] Stress can account for a variety of diseases, as well as lowered immunity, and can itself be generated by a variety of physical and psychosocial stimuli. (The neuroendocrinological changes that constitute this nonspecific physiological response and the effects of prolonged uninterrupted stress on the body will be reviewed later.)[9] Eyer argues that "excessive" (or surplus) stress[10] is integral to capitalist social structure with its various dislocations and disruptions (for example, unemployment), which have their origins in capitalism's economic cycles. Stress is also the product of time-pressured work and a competitiveness that is not only a response to job pressures, but is internalized and encouraged as a personal style in the socialization process of capitalist and similarly production-oriented, societies, such as the U.S.S.R.).[11] This process encourages

[8]I place symptoms in quotes since, strictly speaking, symptoms are what are reported by the patient, while signs are what the doctor observes.

[9]A response is nonspecific in that the same response can be evoked by a great variety of stimuli.

[10]All societies produce stress, though some probably produce more stress than others. The society that generates the least stress necessary to produce a comfortable existence (in the context of its physical-geographical environment and relative to the sophistication of its productive forces) does not exist, but this does not preclude its possibility. I assume (along with Eyer) that the high level of sophistication of productive forces in modern capitalist societies is not commensurate with the high level of work stress imposed by these productive forces. Excessive stress, I believe, is caused to a great extent by hierarchical relationships that affect, among other things, control over productive forces and distribution of their fruits. In other words, our vast potential to provide forces us to measure ourselves against what *could* be, not against past societies, which may or may not have been more repressive. Life may be better now that it was under feudalism, but that does not excuse the barbarities that persist today.

[11]Eyer points out that similar mortality-morbidity patterns (for example, high rates of coronary heart disease, hypertension) prevail in the socialist countries of Eastern Europe. In these societies, as in monopoly capitalist societies, the thrust is toward "the efficient accumulation of capital" (Eyer and Sterling, 1977: 38). As Braverman (1974) noted, the Soviets eagerly appropriated capitalist techniques of increasing labor productivity (e.g., the assembly line). Monopoly or "modern capitalism," whether dominated by a state bureaucracy or by private interests, is thus characterized by centralized

individuals to develop "coronary prone" styles of dealing with the world.

While hypertension occurs disproportionately among such oppressed groups as black males, it is also very prevalent among professional classes as well (Eyer, 1975). Schnall and Kern (1981: 107), whose review of studies on hypertension in American society reaches conclusions similar to Eyer's, point out that Eyer is limited by his "puzzling conclusion" that there is no relationship between blood pressure and economic level of the population or family income. In contrast, they try to show that in fact a strong relationship does exist between hypertension and social class. In fairness to Eyer, however, he does acknowledge a relationship between extremes, that is, between being very rich or very poor and having high blood pressure, and merely states that the relationship between social class and hypertension is not clearcut. What he is trying to emphasize is that the sickening consequences of social structures such as capitalism are not restricted to one class. Such patterns as "coronary prone" behavior (e.g., the Type A personality) are clearly not limited to the lower class, but affect professionals and executives as well. Schnall and Kern (1981) also indicate that there is a link between hypertension and sex. Women over the age of 45 show a higher blood pressure than men of a similar age. The two authors view the increased blood pressure associated with age in our society as a result of accumulated stress and the powerless position of the aged in our society—an inter-

---

large-scale production and technology (for example, nuclear power), by the highly rationalized regulation of the productive process, which emphasizes productivity over the quality of life, by a lack of worker control and by discontinuities between consumption, management-planning, and productive functions. Some readers will object that this comparison with the Soviet system obscures important differences, but I feel it is important to highlight the fact that the human-oriented socialism envisioned by Marx and others has not yet emerged.

pretation with which I concur. Yet ironically, though women are a sociological minority that is, a minority in terms of social power, not in terms of numbers, and though their morbidity rates are higher than men, their life expectancy, despite current social changes, remains considerably higher than that of men.

Waldron (1976) argues (and I share her conclusion) that, though genetic factors may explain some of these sex differences, behavioral patterns characteristic of males are also important factors. These include the "coronary prone pattern" of behavior more common to men. While I do not deny the "obvious" connection between class or other forms of social power and morbidity and mortality, in this essay I hope to expand and refine the explanatory power of theories that see disease and illness as "socially produced" (Conrad and Kern, 1981) by socioeconomic domination. Eyer's conclusion ceases to be "puzzling" when one focuses on the health effects of one specific use of power—*social control.*

How do forms of social control integral to modern societies contribute to morbidity, mortality and to susceptibility to disease? Apart from the neuroendocrinological effects on the body called stress, are there other adverse physiological consequences which are produced by various social control measures? The framework for my analysis will not be limited to the economic sphere, which is but one system of domination. Racism, sexism and ageism intertwine with and mutually reinforce other systems of domination in our society and must be considered. What part is played in the "social production" of disease and illness by one's social experience in the private sphere and such institutions as the family?

There are many structural sources of illness and disease which subject individuals to various kinds of powerlessness. As Eyer and others demonstrate, for instance, morbidity and mortality can be affected by the market fluctuations and economic cycles of capitalism (e.g., the stress of social dislocation, unemployment, etc.)[12] Structurally induced pressures (i.e. relegating women into isolating "housewife" roles) can also affect the degree of social isolation that individuals experience. A lack of social networks of support can have an impact on one's health (see, for instance, Lynch, 1979). So, a variety and interaction of structural factions conspire and assault an individual's "bodily regulation" on a number of flanks. (See Gore, 1978). Other factors are clearly significant, but fall outside of the range of those sources of wear and tear that I consider, and thus I make no claims at providing an exhaustive explanation of the social sources of illness and disease.

SOCIAL CONTROL

To talk about social control is to refer ultimately to ways in which a "society" (dominated by specific class and other shared interests) assures itself of proper respectable behavior and controls the productivity of (and, increasingly, the consumer spending by) its members.[13] Social control mechanisms assure a relatively smooth-functioning social order and maintenance of extant hierarchical arrangements. Such control relies on violence, force, persuasion and manipulation. Control can be "internalized" (and thus self-initiated) as well as externally imposed.

[12]For different interpretations of the relationship between fluctuations of employment rates and health, see Eyer (1977; 1979), and Cooper (1979). An example of a comparative study of the effects of unemployment in Western industrial societies can also be found in Brenner's work (1979). Other worthwhile sources include Liem (1981), whose review of the literature focuses mainly on mental illness, and Navarro (1976).

[13]Janowitz (1975) traces the shifting usage of the concept of social control in sociological theory over the years. He argues that it initially referred to social regulation but more recently it has been used to refer to the means of insuring social conformity and controlling deviance. The recent emphasis has been on socialization and social repression. He suggests a return to the initial usage. In this essay, however, I favor the recent usage, since to think of social control as "societal self-regulation" tends to obscure the contexts of inequality in which such control occurs.

Social control under any conditions can be repressive, but under conditions of social domination it produces a "surplus" of repression. (For a definition of "surplus repression," see Marcuse, 1955: 32.) Thus, it will be assumed that while social control is not synonymous with domination and operates in all social structures, its degree, intensity and form are affected by social relationships of domination. Under such conditions, effects of social control on the individual become intensified.

What are some of the ways in which social control measures affect health? This is the central question to be considered in the pages that follow. While social scientists have studied medical institutions as agencies of social control and the effect of social control on health care delivery (Waitzkin and Waterman, 1974), the consequences of such control for health itself have been touched upon only indirectly.[14] The concept of social control parsimoniously links power to health, since there is a need to control the behavior, attitudes and physical bodies not only of those who are dominated but of the dominators as well. The means of social control may differ in emphasis—may be internalized or externalized—but both parties in a relationship of domination must be subject to control. I am not minimizing the relationship between

---

[14]Two such studies are Zola's (1972) excellent article on medicine as an institution of social control and, more recently, Conrad and Schneider's (1980) in-depth study of the increasing medicalization of life and its implications for social control. Zola sees medical institutions as increasingly important agents of social control, replacing or including in their jurisdiction "traditional" agents such as religious and legal institutions. It is clear that in their role as mystifiers of social oppression and "depoliticizers" of everyday life, medical institutions affect bodily regulation.

The sickening effects of social control practices are particularly pronounced in two types of institutions—those one is "attached" to (for instance, the family) and those that make human beings objects to work on (total institutions, such as hospitals or clinics, and welfare agencies). It is the second type of institution that is the source of many of my illustrations since this type brings to the fore in an almost caricatured fashion the relationship between social structure, control and health. I focus (with some exceptions) on intra-institutional forms of control. These may well bear a resemblance to each other from institution to institution. Work imposes time discipline, but so does school life, partly to prepare one for work.

extreme forms of powerlessness and health, but merely attempting to refine the connections. I believe the consequences of domination for *both* oppressor and oppressed have been neglected. For instance, the system of domination called sexism (to mention one of many systems!) not only assaults the female body but deprives males, as well, of full partnership with their bodies. Our society takes away a woman's bodily proprietary rights and transforms her into a commoditized sex object. But men also pay a price by not being able to express their emotions, and not being able to acknowledge the need to rest or to abandon the constant body vigilance which is supported by masculine values and social situations that demand competitiveness.

Appropriating the mind simply through socialization practices, or manipulating social information (e.g., symbols), does not guarantee the maintenance of productivity levels or give the assurance that social actors will maintain normal, appropriate appearances. Social control also operates physically on the body through, for instance, inhibiting impulses to play at various times or to display inappropriate emotions or gestures and by influencing the very rhythm in which the body is allowed to go through its paces. Such body discipline, while an essential prerequisite to social existence, can nonetheless have destructive effects on the organism.[15] This, one assumes, is particularly true when the organism is subject to mobilization in the interests of domination and exploitation.

Social control includes not only these types of control of the body, but is, in itself, also capable of undermining the

---

[15]It is understood, of course, that body discipline per se is not the issue, since, after all, increasing "orderliness of muscular control" (Antonovsky, 1979: 120) is one of the means by which a person survives. There are, however, unnecessarily stressful, uncomfortable, or over-inhibiting forms of control, and it is to these that I refer. Bourgeois body etiquette includes a strong "fart" taboo which, it may be argued, can be related to intestinal disorders (Rabkin and Silberman, 1979). We should be cautious in making much of this example, but the relationship between bodily control and health is only now beginning to get attention.

capacity of the body to "control" itself in a way essential to the maintenance of a high level of health. Even when this control is not directly physical, it can nonetheless affect the body's governance over its inner and outer environment.

A NOTE ON THE COGNITIVE BIAS OF SOCIAL SCIENTISTS

Sociologists, as one might expect, tend to ignore the body and to "desomatize" social relationships. Even those who have looked at the relationship of society to the human body have tended to see this relationship from an idealist perspective. Most theories that look at social sources of sickness tend to employ different versions of "cognitive" models. Moss, for example, views "informational incongruity" (1973)—the dissonance generated by, for instance, a contradiction between one's personal expectations and their realization—as leading to imbalances or a loss of regulation in the integration of different parts of the nervous system. He calls this state "tuning" which leads to a lowered immunity to disease. Others, such as Antonovsky (1979), suggest that a lack of a "sense of coherence"—the experience of one's world as manageable and under reasonable control—constitutes a cognitive source of disease. The most recent formulations of a general social theory of disease can be found in Totman's *Social Causes of Illness* (1979). In this work it is "social disorientation"—a lack of clear rules or structure, that has adverse neuroendocrinological consequences for the human organism. These approaches, share in common their failure to see these various forms of dissonance, disorientation, etc. as being intrinsic features of systems of social domination. They also tend to reduce social pressures to noncorporeal forms. For instance, conformity to arbitrary authority requires not only a certain attitude or generates dissonance but also strict control of such forms of bodily expression as anger. Invalidating an individual may involve not merely an attack on one's definition of self but on the control of one's body. These cognitive approaches view social order as primarily a network of symbolic exchanges—a web of information and ideas (Moss, 1973). To conceive of order in this way does not allow for consideration of the "material" pressures that buffet the body in its movement through social space. Society becomes ethereal, a mental chimera in which the social actor is desomatized, stripped of emotion, viscera and muscles and turned into an information-processing machine. This perspective is not so much incorrect as partial. Indeed, society is, among other things, an informational network, and "dissonant" information *does* have physiological consequences for the body. Informational "troubles," I argue later, are essential consequences of social control measures that are part and parcel of systems of domination. These informational troubles assault the body's ability to regulate itself, but are by no means the only sources that assault bodily regulation.

Social control also influences the tempo of life, the motions of the body, and the degree to which "impulses" can be expressed in bodily behavior. The idealist perspective, with its exclusive emphasis on cognition and perception, shifts attention away from sickening social structures towards individual actors and their sickening ways of perceiving, thinking and responding to their world.

CIVILIZED SOCIAL CONTROL

Just as systems of domination change historically, so do their means of social control. These means are thus no more static than the historically changing economic and social life that they support. The ways in which individuals have been governed and pressured to conform have changed with the ascendancy of industrial capitalism and, in the twentieth century, with monopoly capitalism. To describe the nature of this change I utilize Gustav Ichheiser's (1970) metaphor of "invisibility." Modern social control, *both in the private [i.e., the family], as well as in the public spheres of life [i.e., work]*, can be characterized by its increasing invisibility. It is the embeddedness of controls "inside" the body, social control as personal internalized control, the reliance on informational manipulation (for instance, propaganda, public relations, etc.) and other forms of "indirect coercion," that constitute its invisibility.

Holistic medicine has a lot to contribute to our understanding of the effects on health of modern social control. It emphasizes that "diseases of civilization" (e.g., cancer, coronary heart disease) are generated by time pressures, by the ambiguity and insecurity of modern life and other aspects of "civilization." From a broader perspective, however, the holistic approach is incomplete because it does not sufficiently recognize that civilization refers, among other things, to forms of social control that sustain a social hierarchy which values productivity over the quality of life.

Several "civilized" forms of control that sustain relationships of domination will be emphasized—those that inhibit the presentation of self or invalidate the individual, and those that regulate time, bodily expression and social information in such a way as to render individuals powerless. These forms of control deprive the body of its regulatory abilities, abilities that in turn sustain an optimum level of health. Social control, for instance, can influence how "in touch" we are with our bodies, by desensitizing us to bodily experience essential to monitoring our state of health, or by making it difficult for our bodies to mobilize healing resources such as the ability to relax. Not being able to relax or "let go" is endemic to our society, and is the result of pressures placed upon us to always be in control. Self-control, to the point of being unable to surrender control, is one of the features of bourgeois "personality" that encourages production and a great deal of self-imposed repression. Weber (1958) originally described the value system that helped form the character of early capitalists; he illuminated sources of contemporary personal traits such as a high degree of self-control and a tendency to delay gratification.

In our society, the ethos of bourgeois individualism and the "civilized" forms of control imposed on us encourage us to believe that the self is at the center of the universe and has the responsibility and ability to move the universe and to endure its onslaughts. On the other hand, many of the external conditions that individuals face in bourgeois society in fact invalidate the individual's potential. We value authenticity and self-worth. Yet social conditions simultaneously attack self-esteem and make the expression of an authentic self difficult. For instance, the hierarchical relationships of class, race, sex and education impose limits on us. The measures that sustain hierarchical relationships are inherently self-denigrating. Assaults on our sense of self, our competence and existential purpose may erode our "will to live." We are broken up and "give up" our bodily "control." Defenses decline and self-healing capacities weaken.

Social control increasingly involves self-imposed restraints over the body and the expression of its impulses. Under certain conditions, such restraints can become the basis of psychosomatic illness. For instance, individuals may be exposed to various kinds of threatening situations, but internal constraints inhibit healthy anger and its somatic correlates.

Our childhood and adult experiences can bow and stiffen us, covering the body with what Reich called a muscular armor. This armor results from the constant stifling of spontaneous bodily impulses.[16] "Retroflection" is the name given

---

[16]It was Wilhelm Reich who first articulated the relationship between macro-sociopolitical structure and body repression. Reich was a socialist who found himself increasingly ostracized by the Left. He focused on the ways social structures (for instance, authoritarian family structure) produced muscular armor or tension, which in turn blocked the flow of sexual-life energy. I prefer to view his concepts more as metaphors than as literal observations. Yet Reich was sensitive to the relationship between patriarchal-capitalist domination (which, to his dismay, existed in a "socialist"

by some Gestalt psychologists to the unresolved psychic tensions that are expressed somatically (Enright, 1970). Such tensions are the result of a habitual inhibition of the spontaneous wishes to play and to be sensuous that surge out of our bodies. The body is put in a perpetual state of muscular tension, becomes unable to accurately experience somatic messages, and is under constant stress. Retroflection is one of the results of a highly refined body etiquette which characterizes civilized bourgeois social control.

Forms of domination such as the work relationships of capitalism also impose corporeal yokes that break the body and infiltrate its interior. Thus, in a "civilized" fashion, individuals do their own yoking. The powerlessness in relation to one's body is produced by the excessive pressures of both external and self-imposed measures of control that are integral to these relationships of domination.

The conditions of work in our society overwhelm our bodies by placing them into environments that move too fast, or sap our energy by placing us into contexts that fail to stimulate. The bodies of workers are thus harnessed to the rhythms of the clock and to the dictates of scientifically managed productivity. The assembly-line worker is the prototype of such yoking. Again, that yoking need not be externally imposed, for the executive (even in the absence of externally imposed necessity) may be driven by a competitiveness, an internal "time sickness" and need to control, which may lead him or her to ignore bodily wisdom and to drive the body at a speed that abuses it. Many executives have remarked at the disorientation they experience when their watches break!

The productive relations of monopoly capitalism are maintained by a highly rationalized, "scientific" control over time and a stringent work discipline. The rhythms of clock time increasingly permeate all aspects of everyday life. Com-

---

country) and bodily functioning (Robinson, 1969). Holistic medicine is in many ways neo-Reichian.

pulsive attitudes towards punctuality and efficient use of time are internalized not only by the bourgeoisie but by workers as well.

Coercion as a form of social control is more and more being replaced by the control over information. Propaganda, public relations and the monopoly over knowledge—by management in the work place, and by the professions in service organizations—have the consequence of inducing powerlessness. Workers, to take one example, have little say in planning, seldom are informed about the rationale behind production quotas or about the future of their jobs. The anxiety produced by a lack of worker control over information may produce a chronic, diffuse stress which, when continued unabated, could undermine the body's internal balance and harmony.

HOLISTIC MEDICINE AND BODILY REGULATION

Holistic or psychological medicine repeatedly emphasizes disease as a loss of bodily regulation. It recognizes the need for patients to assume "responsibility" for their bodies. I make use of its literature to support my claims about the relationship between social and bodily "control" and health. Unfortunately, only some of the more "politicized" practitioners of holistic medicine have recognized the strong connection between political order, civilization and bodily regulation. Feminist writers on health, who draw on holistic theory, are particularly aware of the ways in which social domination deprives one of bodily "control." *Seizing Our Bodies, Our Bodies, Our Selves,* and *Vaginal Politics* are all titles of feminist books on health that express this connection. Women have become increasingly conscious of external (and internalized) forms of bodily domination as well as ways in which their bodies are "colonized" through, for instance, the acceptance of self-destructive body images and physical norms. One of the aims of women's liberation, in general, and the women's health movement, in particular, is the emancipation of the body from male domination. Some of the contemporary pioneering work on health and power relations comes from feminist sources, as do alternative structures and models for health care. My emphasis is on the ways that social measures of control encourage the body to ignore its own wisdom, to push itself beyond its capacities—in short, the ways in which social control interferes with the body's capacity to function optimally. The chapters that follow examine the consequences of modern social control for bodily wear and tear, for the maintenance of the body's defenses, and for the body's ability to monitor its external and internal environments. In the next chapter I more closely examine the contributions of holistic medicine, especially that of feminists (who have used holistic theory), to the notion of bodily regulation as an integral feature of health. This chapter is followed by an elaboration of some of the physiological consequences of a lack of regulation, as well as some of the methodological problems involved in studying these consequences. I then examine the relationship of the individual to social control forces. The remaining chapters of this essay look at the "invisible" nature of modern social control and then describe the effects of this control on health.

CHAPTER TWO

Holistic Medicine and Re-Claiming the Body

THE HOLISTIC CRITIQUE

What has been called "psychological" (Bakal, 1979), "non-allopathic" (Weil, 1973), or "holistic" (Pelletier, 1977) medicine has in the past two decades provided a challenge to the prevailing biomedical paradigm. Its advocates include those outside or on the fringes of conventional medicine as well as an increasing minority within both the medical establishment[1] and in the discipline of psychology. The holistic approach to health provides a broader or more "holistic" version of health which includes psychosocial components; it sees the lack of integration of various mind-body functions as sickening or as making us more vulnerable to sickness. In many ways, its stress on avoiding monocausal explanations and its emphasis on the significance of the "subjective" dimensions of health can be seen as a methodological revolt against medical positivism. (See, for example, Shealy, 1979.)

[1]This includes, on the whole, younger physicians who are breaking with traditional ways. There now exists an American Holistic Medical Association, and holistic approaches are supported by prominent researchers such as Hans Selye ("Is Holistic Political?").

Health is not viewed simply as the absence of clinically visible symptoms or disease but involves different degrees of general well being (Ahmed and Coelho, 1979). Health and disease are on a *continuum* that ranges from serious break-down in bodily functioning (what Symes calls "brokenness," as cited in Twaddle and Hessler, 1977: 73) to states of extraordinary vigor and a feeling of well-being.

When does the process of being unhealthy begin? Does it begin when clinically objective signs, or subjectively felt symptoms appear? Does it begin at a subclinical threshold not discernible to a clinical medical establishment more oriented to disease than health?

> It is frequently difficult to ascertain when a disease begins. Most diseases are the culmination of long-term biological adaptations to the internal and external environment. Although symptoms may not appear until much later in life, biological study will demonstrate deterioration of body organs over many years. Although coronary heart disease does not usually occur until we reach the 50s and 60s, autopsy studies of children and young soldiers who died of causes other than heart disease indicate that many of them already have considerable evidence of atherosclerosis (arterial deposits of cholesterol, fats and other substances). Thus, although an infarction is a discrete and easily identifiable event, the underlying process contributing to it begins at an early age. In the cases of many chronic diseases such as rheumatoid arthritis, renal failure, and diabetes, symptoms progress over a period of years, and it is even more difficult to identify the occurrence of a new case, although the first diagnosis is usually used as the appropriate criterion. (Mechanic, 1978A: 137)

The fact of "subclinical illness" means that prevalence data and statistical correlations that are found between specific illnesses and social conditions must be treated with a great deal of caution. Conversely, the absence of a clinically visible link between these factors cannot be taken as definitive. In political terms, there are many implications of limiting one's attention to the appearance of clinically visible symptoms.

An outstanding example is the workplace. First of all, only those who are visibly broken become the focus of interest, with the implication that those workers who do not *visibly* "break" under the pressures of an environment are healthy. Secondly, given the fact that not all *appear* ill, one can be misled into limiting one's analysis to *individual susceptibility*, not to the noxious stimuli in the workplace. This is the tack of self-interested company representatives and insurance companies that seek to limit workmen's compensation claims and company liability (Berman, 1979).

Health, in the holistic framework, refers to a state of optimum functioning, or, as Kass suggests, a "well-working" organism whose activity is "in accordance with its specific excellences" (1975: 29). Engel (1969: 240) offers a number of compelling reasons for adapting a broad conceptualization of health (or disease) as optimal (or poor) functioning. Such a conceptualization emphasizes a multifactor approach, it does not fix one's attention on a narrow level of analysis, like intracellular functioning, and it discourages the assumption that health or disease are properties independent of the patient. Holistic definitions of health presuppose "natural" standards that transcend particular sociohistorical contexts. In contrast, Dingwall and others (1976) argue that health and disease are social constructions not found in a state of nature. It is true that disability and disease can be viewed as context dependent, and thus symptoms of arthritis, for instance, are more or less noticeable or incapacitating in relation to the specific social context. Yet it is also true that the state of impaired functioning produced by this disease of the joints nonetheless exists as an objective physical fact. What a naively relativistic definition of health misses is that it is not the existence of a dichotomous state of health or non-health that is relative, but the importance, noticeability, etc., of these bodily states due to differing situations, demands and expectations (Kass, 1975).

The standards for such a definition can only be derived from a living organism in action, not, as Kass says, from a "statue" (1975: 27). One type of norm involves parameters for the working of certain bodily processes such as blood pressure, clotting speed, temperature, salt and potassium, or electrolyte functioning. These types of norms, though somewhat variable from organism to organism and even changing for an individual (e.g., blood pressure depends on the time of day), nonetheless have parameters of excess and deficiency. When blood pressure rises too high, the body acts to bring it back to reasonable limits (Kass, 1975). The body sets into motion equilibrating forces in order to restore homeostasis (Cannon, 1968).

Those norms are not the only standards for a well-functioning body. There are also those that fall under the heading of mind-body integration. Most of medical research recognizes the significance of the first type of norm, but it is in holistic approaches where the second type of norm, mind-body integration, is important. Such an integration allows the body to mobilize its healing and immune responses and allows the body to accurately process bodily information such as pain.

The core assumptions of "holism" in medicine emphasize the need to look at the whole patient—not separate mind and body or the context in which the patient is found. Pain, for instance, is neither organic nor "all in the mind" but psyche and soma influencing each other, in a complex interrelationship. Stress and tension may induce muscular spasm, which aggravates and prolongs pain and other symptoms in many illnesses; physical distress further induces stress and tension. The goal of holistic medicine is to "heal" the mind-body split that deprives individuals of the ability to experience and control the body (Gordon, 1980: 16). Treating the experience that a person has of a disease and the quality of the person's life are, therefore, as important as treating the disease itself (Kleinman, 1978). These holistic goals are based on the awareness that humans are "open systems" in constant interaction with both their inner and outer environments (Gordon, 1980: 16). The patient and the patient's surroundings are viewed ecologically, as a unit, and thus daily personal and social problems, diet, and other factors become important.

THE LIMITS OF BOURGEOIS HOLISTIC MEDICINE

Despite the sensitivity of holistic approaches to environmental factors, most practitioners do little to attempt to change the environment but resort instead to individualistic treatments such as rolfing, biofeedback, etc. While the purpose of these treatments is to try to restore bodily control, little is done to systematically or structurally change the conditions that led to the loss of such control in the first place. Recommendations that one take up yoga, meditation or change one's attitude towards time show an insensitivity to the realities of social class differences. Friedman and Rosenman (1974), the authors of *Type A Behavior and Your Heart,* an important source in holistic medicine, exemplify this naiveté about class (*New York Times Book Review*, May 19, 1974, p. 9). For instance, the authors recommend that "you" (as if all of their readers are executives and members of the middle class) fire your secretary if "she" does not have a Type B personal style or is unwilling to change. Such a suggestion ignores the pressures that engulf secretaries who, in fact, often act as buffers for their bosses. One cheerfully titled book, *The Holistic Way to Health and Happiness* (Bloomfield, 1978), tells "you" to change attitude as to time and then talk to your boss about alleviating time pressure and how you feel about your job. If you do this, your boss will respect you; if not, change your job: excellent advice for an auto worker with a family to support at a time of high unemployment! The connection between social and political hierarchy and the "sick person" is largely glossed over. References to the environment use essentially middle-class euphemisms such as "lifestyle," which, like fashion, can presumably be changed at will. The ability and willingness to change are often seen merely as a matter of the right attitude or technique (Berliner and Salmon, 1979). Many of the solutions advocated by holistic medicine have been appropriately described as "Buddhist solutions" by Eyer (1975)—ones that advocate withdrawal and are more suited to professional and managerial classes who possess the control over their environments that make such solutions possible. In other cases, holistic medicine recognizes the reality of external pressures such as time, but possibilities of concerted action to effect political and social change are ignored. Instead, the patient feels encouraged to accept such pressures, to view attitudinal reactions as the key, and to adjust through the medium of such individual changes as the "relaxation response." Thus, according to Benson, the rapid pace of life is not expected to slow down since our standard of living depends on that pace; and, he adds, "it is unlikely most executives would want it to slow down" (1979: 334–335).

Most holism is easily absorbed into the structure of capitalism and readily adopts its values and language without recognizing the ultimate contradiction between profit, a lack of worker control, and health. Corporations are increasingly willing to include meditation, relaxation and exercise into their programs (at least for executives), provided these programs aid productivity. A recent article entitled "Corporate Wellness Programs: Good Health is Good Business" (Jennings and Tager, 1981) tells us that some companies have meditation rooms ("complete with Zen pillows") as well as "modules" on weight loss, stress management, and other components of the healthy "lifestyle." Executives or workers interested in wellness are not asked to reevaluate basic goals and principles. The authors conclude that "the effort to create a healthy American work life cannot succeed unless those capable of administering high quality programs can *sell* them. To do that business must be met on its own turf, convinced in its own language and motivated to act on the basis of its own values"(ibid.: 18). In a truly healthy workplace, however, the bottom line cannot always be productivity. Such programs can ameliorate stress and help, in a piecemeal fashion, to repair damaged human "commodities." They do not encourage (in fact, they *discourage*, by co-opting workers) concerted political action and the fundamental restructuring of productive relations necessary for meeting human needs and improving the quality of the working day. Such changes would entail, for instance, redesigning office or factory spaces so there is provision for periodic physical movement, change of position, and environmental conditions that are more pleasant and aesthetic (for instance, greenery, fresh air and non-glaring lights), thereby reducing stress.

The holistic approach does take note of social factors by alluding to the effects of "modern society," "urban way of life," "competitiveness," or "civilization" (Berliner and Salmon, 1979: 45). Such concepts as "civilization" are treated as reified processes independent of the social structures in which they exist. As in many contemporary sociological analyses, the power arrangements that encourage these problems (such as "a harried way of life") are seldom articulated. Much like the editorial "we" in "we pollute," such general terms as "civilization" tend to conceal the power arrangements that lie at their core.

There are times when advocates of "holism" display by neglect an unwittingly conservative attitude towards social change and a blind spot to the sickening aspects of the status quo. Pelletier, a sophisticated advocate of the holistic approach, provides an example. Discussing women's liberation, he focuses only on the stressful aspects of change. Women feel pressures to abandon traditional roles, and men may begin to feel insecure as a result of the challenge to their preeminence. Men may feel seriously threatened and under stress (1977: 88). Here he reflects a bias that is typical not only of holistic approaches but of "bourgeois" sociology in general. The fact then that health seems to improve during periods of class struggle appears, as Berliner and Salmon put it, "somewhat of a mystery to bourgeois medical understanding" (1979: 47–48). At no time does Pelletier hint at the sickening aspects for women inherent in their deprived secondary social position or the stressful consequences of sexism for men themselves. The bias towards the healing consequences of order and stability also leads Pelletier to view fixed social hierarchies in which "everyone knows their place" as salutogenic. He is not so attentive to the quality (as opposed to simple stability and security) of class relationships that are essentially relationships of domination. The existential quality of one's particular place in a hierarchy comes to be viewed as secondary, and Pelletier works from essentially conservative assumptions that take for granted the social order's predominance over individual needs. A solution to tensions between social structures and individuals is to learn to "accept" that structure. (In this respect, he approaches society the same way as most sociologists!)

Many advocates of the holistic approach are aware of the "disabling" consequences of conventional approaches to medical healing (though they do not pay enough attention to the "disabling" consequences of other institutionalized relationships, such as work). It is an important part of holistic ideology that patients be active participants in the healing process, that they be able to mobilize themselves, and, in a sense, take responsibility for their bodies. It is for this and other reasons that many writers in holistic medicine welcome Illich's critique of medical institutions. Illich et al. (1977) argues that one of the iatrogenic (medically induced) consequences of these institutions is dependency in their clients. He does not, however, sufficiently stress the fact that such dependency is partly the result of social control measures (dependent role, monopoly over knowledge, and others) that sustain the large gap between "expert" and "client." Furthermore, the fee-for-service system, in which even holistic practitioners participate, produces pressures to increase medical productivity at the patient's expense or even to create medical problems. Such a financial arrangement is both costly to the patient and fosters a vested interest in repeated and unnecessary service (Waitzkin and Waterman, 1974).

The commoditization process, which I shall describe later, penetrates into the deepest layers of everyday life and is increasingly pervasive in contemporary capitalist societies. Health is no less a commodity for holistic medicine than for the medical industrial complex. The Body—lean, tanned, with a healthy mane of hair, brimming with animal vigor—is a very salable image in a society that makes Youth a fetish. Holistic medicine capitalizes on this dream by offering packaged health in the form of vitamins, organic food, endless do-it-yourself manuals and catalogues, courses on reflexology, and so on.

Such a partial approach offers the often false prospect of a healthy mind-body, but only to those who have the time and especially money to explore these alternatives. More significantly, this dream is parceled and sold in a piecemeal fashion—by the hour, pound, consultation, or specific technique. Each institute, distributor, merchant, healer-guru offers one approach (often at the exclusion of others). One can jog take courses, be counseled, buy herbs, balms, hot tubs, and even go to a weekend spa. But neglected is the necessity of restructuring the deeper social realities that limit access to (or the realization of) this dream. The unhealthy home, workplace, and urban environment (and, above all, its macro-social contexts) remain untouched. In short, holistic medicine cannot be truly "whole" as long as it is offered as part of an anarchic, fragmenting marketplace and not as part of a unified approach that includes change on a macro-social scale *as well as* in one's everyday life.

THE RADICAL SENSIBILITY AMONG HOLISTIC PRACTITIONERS

Some holistic practitioners who were a part of the counter-culture of the sixties became radically politicized in that period, and this political consciousness left its mark. They show an awareness not only of the need for the individual to control his or her body but the necessity for that control to be reappropriated. They see the need to liberate the body from the bonds of subtle and pervasive bonds of social oppression that have increasingly revealed themselves to them in the course of their social experience. Grossinger sums up this awareness most forcefully:

> As it became clear that it was impossible to overthrow the system and that the system had gotten into one's guts and cells, the important thing became to change oneself to make oneself into a new person, an actual revolutionary who purges the somatic-psychic fact of having been born and raised in the belly of the giant. (1980: 339)

The individualistic ideology described earlier as characterizing the approach of many of those in holistic medicine (and in the sociology of health and illness) therefore does not characterize the entire community of holistic practitioners. Many of them, though they rely on such individualistic techniques as "rolfing" to reintegrate muscular functioning, recognize, much as did Wilhelm Reich, whose work had a strong influence on "rolfing theory," that muscular and character armor have political and social sources that need to be changed. The difficulty in trying to reappropriate bodily control in contexts that dominate the body are thus recognized. *Both* "individual" and "social" changes are essential for any health "revolution."

Similarly, some holistic advocates have recognized the limits of the emphasis on the individual as self-healer. Thus, one lesbian feminist practitioner explains both the dangers as well as radicalizing potential of this emphasis:

> One of the benefits of holistic health is that it allows people to move beyond the passive role too often perpetuated by conventional medical practice in American culture. To take responsibility for one's body is to begin to see the connection between sickness and political oppression. The danger lies in taking responsibility to the point of ignoring the political realities that caused the problem. ("Is Holistic Political?" p. 9)

There are those practitioners who have found in holistic practice an alternative to what was experienced as sexism in conventional medical practice, such as excluding women healers or invalidating women patients. Beginning in the 1970s, many women organized referral networks. In Berkeley, California, a system of feedback on doctors and their relationship with women patients was established. Health clinics run by women and based on holistic principles and on self-care began to emerge. Midwives challenged the monopoly over medical knowledge and the tendency to view pregnancy as a disease. Not only did many women turn to holistic medicine with this awareness, but the practice of holistic medicine *in and of itself* increased that awareness. In fact, it is women, for whom a central part of their oppression has been the male domination of their bodies, who are the most conscious of the conditions that deprive individuals of such control. In the introduction to the book *Seizing Our Bodies*, Claudia Dreifus argues that what unites the women's health movement is the fact that knowing one's body can be liberating and that women must insist on controlling "the means of reproduction"—their bodies.[2]

> In editing the collection, I have asked the question 'who controls a woman's body and why?' Moreover, I've sought to tell the story of the women who call themselves health feminists, those pioneers of self knowledge and self determination. *Seizing Our Bodies* is meant as a guidebook to a social revolution: it is not the factories or postoffices that are being seized but the limbs and organs of the human beings who own them. (1978: xxxi)

Holistic medicine, with its focus on everyday life, can offer some of the tools and the politically radicalizing consciousness that are needed for initiating such a revolution; it can

---

[2]In a similar vein, Goldberg (1976: 111) suggests that bodily liberation is a prerequisite for male liberation: "In general, the liberation of the male consciousness is particularly predicated on the liberation of the male body. A man whose physical awareness is inhibited by guilt, who relies on his wife to 'take care of him,' who is out of touch with, distrustful and unmindful of his body's signals, who intellectualizes rather than responds to his body's messages, who represses his emotions and pays the price in terms of psychosomatic illnesses and who maintains rigid macho habit patterns in relation to both males and females, is on a path of self-destruction."

sensitize us to new levels and nuances of social oppression. Yet, observers from the left, such as Berliner and Salmon (1979), with their orthodox Marxist perspective, fail to see this potential. Their critiques of the social order neglect the sphere of everyday life and other forms of oppression such as ageism and often sexism, and they remain blind to those "invisible" bonds that bind the body and blind to holistic medicine's potential both to bring these bonds into view and to loosen them.

Holistic medicine points to the important relationship of power to health, but, unfortunately, it often loses sight of the structural sources of powerlessness that impose limits on one's ability to take control of one's body. My essay attempts to call attention to these structural sources of powerlessness. "Psychological" medicine must go beyond itself and uncritical "bourgeois" characterizations of the social order that beset much sociological thinking and writing. This is the task here, and it is an essential one for a sociology of health and illness.

I now turn to the physiological bases of bodily deregulation and the effects of such deregulation on health. After looking at the relationship of the individual actor to forms of social control, I review some of the forms of social control that characterize modern bourgeois social relationships, both in the private and public spheres. The remaining chapters look at some of the contemporary sources of bodily powerlessness.

CHAPTER THREE

The Physiological Bases of Bodily Deregulation

BODILY REGULATION

Very few sociologists (myself certainly included) possess the background in both sociology and medicine to be able to draw the connection between social conditions and the biological mechanisms activating health and illness. Moss is one of the few social scientists who also has a background in the biological sciences. He correctly states that the "first task for scientists having some competence in both social and biological fields is to develop researchable and refutable conceptual frameworks" (1973: 3). Some comments are therefore in order that specify how the loss of bodily regulation translates itself into adverse physiological consequences. The evidence that I cite is illustrative, suggestive and certainly not definitive. The relationships sketched are at times speculative and may often sound a bit more "mechanical" than I actually intend. This mechanical appearance possibly is the result of my effort to be as clear as possible in presenting materials and my dependence on the existing body of literature that often does study those relationships mechanically.

In the previous sections, two interrelated norms for bodily regulation were mentioned. The first of these involved norms for the adequate functioning of various physiological systems. In order to operate, the body must regulate, for instance, blood pressure, body temperature, hormonal levels, electrolyte balance, etc., which must be maintained within parameters that demarcate conditions of excess or deficiency. Equilibrium is maintained by keeping the body in homeostasis. Walter B. Cannon, who first articulated the notion of homeostasis, defined it as follows: "The coordinated physiological processes which maintain most of the steady states in the organism are so complex and so peculiar to living beings—involving, as they may, the brain and nerves, the heart, lungs, kidneys and spleen, all working cooperatively—that I have suggested a special designation for these states, homeostasis" (1968: 258). In Cannon's model the organism is viewed as an open system constantly interacting with changing environmental demands; when environmental pressures are overwhelming and unremitting, homeostasis is disrupted. There are many homeostatic mechanisms: the studies that link psychosocial conditions to health in large measure have focused on the effect of disrupted endocrinological homeostasis on health. This effect will be analyzed in greater depth here.

The second type of norm for wellness, mentioned earlier, involves an integration of mind and body. The relationship between the body's way of communicating with itself and its environment and the effect of the disruption of such communication on health will also be examined here. I will delineate the ways in which being "in touch with one's body" may literally affect health. Being "in touch" refers to the body's ability to monitor and actually interpret messages that come from within (e.g., pain) and also being able to mobilize its resources and evoke its natural "automatic" responses, such as Benson's (1979) "relaxation response."

NEUROENDOCRINOLOGICAL DEREGULATION

The most familiar formulation of the relationship between environmental stressors, a loss of endocrinological homeostasis and a breakdown in physical functioning comes from the work of Hans Selye, who was a student of Walter B. Cannon. The response of the body to the spectrum of environmental demands takes the form of a complex set of endocrinological changes which he calls stress.[1]

Selye identifies two classes of hormones—those that speed up the body and those that slow it down (Wu, 1973: 93). Most subsequent theories that have dealt with the effect of prolonged and excessive stressors on health have built on Selye's assumptions and framework.

Stressful conditions that generate endocrinological "speed up" of the body may eventually upset the ability to "slow down." Similarly, alternating between "high speed" and "low speed" may also destroy endocrinological homeostasis with consequences for immunity, blood pressure and cholesterol production. The prolonged output of catecholamines (adrenal excretions) can lead to the hypo- or hyperdysfunction of one or more organ systems (Kagan and Levi,

---

[1]In *The Stress of Life* (1956), Selye identifies what he calls a "general adaptation syndrome" (G.A.S.) which is a general bodily stress response (in addition to the specific bodily reaction) to any number of physiological stimuli (a change or threat): the pituitary gland secretes ACTH, an "executive" hormone, which in turn stimulates other glands (including the adrenal cortex). These endocrinological changes activate a "primitive" coping pattern of the body—"a fight or flight" stress response. While adaptive energy necessary to deal with a stressor is thereby provided, other bodily operations, such as the immune response, are weakened. If such stress continues, the immune system, not having an opportunity to recoup itself, suffers. Furthermore, the limited store of adaptive energy is depleted, which leads to exhaustion and eventually death. Stressors (whether positive or negative) are the wear and tear of life. Our responses to stress aid survival, but simultaneously wear out the body. If intensive wear and tear continues unremittingly, and the body is not given an opportunity to rest, the stress response leads to a premature destruction of the body's immune system and of the body itself.

1974: 228). Persistent increases in catecholamine activity have been linked to lower immunity to infectious diseases (Gruchow, 1979). Competitive, time-obsessed, Type A behavior, as defined by Friedman and Rosenman (1974), is seen, among other things, as affecting the output of catecholamines. A lack of homeostasis in catecholamine output has also been connected to hypertension (Nixon, 1979).

Homeostasis may be affected not only by an increase or a dramatic lowering in the production of hormones, but by a rapid shuttling between high and low levels. Glass (1977), for instance, argues that the Type A personality in responding to conditions of helplessness alternates frantically between trying to assert control and giving up. Each extreme response produces an attendant rapid rise and lowering of catecholamine excretions. Jolting shifts between sympathetic and parasympathetic nervous system activity and the related rise and fall of catecholamines can be linked to the etiology of coronary heart disease (Glass, 1977: 185).

Thus one type of bodily deregulation that can generate coronary heart disease, hypertension, ulcers, etc., is endocrinological. It involves sustained speeding up or slowing down of the body (or rapid shifts in these speeds) that, if sustained over a period, upset homeostasis with the consequence that the body experiences excessive wear and tear and an assault on its immunity.

Recognition of the importance of endocrinological homeostasis leads us naturally to focus next on some of the ways in which the state of a body's communication with its external and internal environment can affect health. The body's communication and "message" network, the nervous system, has an "automatic" component that regulates, among other things, the above-mentioned endocrinological functions. When, for instance, the sympathetic autonomic nervous system is aroused, endocrinological changes associated with stress are elicited. Continued and extensive sympathetic nervous system arousal not only may create endocrinological disruption, but may affect the nervous system's arousal itself. For instance, sympathetic arousal may eventually dominate and overshadow parasympathetic activity that elicits the "relaxation response," which Benson (1979) sees as the physiological opposite of the stress response.

Several authors have argued that unregulated arousal of one component of the nervous system (which in turn has hormonal consequences) can lead to lowered immunity and disease. "Undampened" sympathetic arousal may make it difficult to adequately manage the muscular system and visceral control. The regulating mechanisms of the body are set "out of whack" if overused: they constantly mobilize the body and do not allow release. This reaction may become "disregulated, protracted and fixed" (Kagan and Levi, 1974: 232). To Moss, a central feature in his explanation of the link between social "informational incongruity" and lowered immunity is the unbalanced arousal of one part of the nervous system. According to him, the nexus between mind and body lies in the balance between the sympathetic and parasympathetic autonomic nervous system. "Informational incongruity" (such as thwarted expectations) creates an imbalance between these systems in which one tends to be predominantly aroused. This condition Moss calls "tuning," and it is linked to changes in the endocrinological system which in turn affect immunity to disease (Moss, 1973). Thus, dissonance-producing information leads to the arousal of the sympathetic nervous system. If sustained, this generates an imbalance in the nervous system ("tuning") with one system "dominating" (Moss, 1973).

It has been pointed out (Kagan and Levi, 1974; Pelletier, 1977) that in "modern" societies, individuals are placed into situations that evoke the "fight or flight" response, but rules of civilized behavior, internal inhibitions, and social pressures do not allow the body to express this response in motor action—by way of some physical reaction—such as fighting, or a direct display of anger, etc. They argue that threatening situations, coupled with "civilized" behavior, encourage bodily deregulation by creating dissociation between emotional expression, neuroendrocrinological accompaniments of emotion, and psychomotor activities that would release the tension (Kagan and Levi, 1974: 230).

Gellhorn (1969) suggests that under "normal" conditions, central nervous system and somatic-muscular arousal generally parallel each other and thus activity in the sympathetic nervous system is accompanied by increased muscle tone. In his review of the literature, Gellhorn finds that the suppression of overt movement (such as motor movements) under conditions of sympathetic arousal leads to a dissociation between nervous system and somatic activity.[2] This in turn deregulates the nervous system and "in the absence of overt movements, the continuation of the ergotropic excitation in the post-stimulating period leads, on repeated exposures, to neuroses" (1969: 298). Thus, when an individual is threatened but cannot fight or give physical expression to his or her emotion, sympathetic activity continues and suppresses the parasympathetic "rebound" that would normally follow and would reestablish homeostasis.[3] Instead, the sympathetic activity continues and eventually "spills over" leading to simultaneous sympathetic-parasympathetic activity. This deregulation in the form of a lack of rebound produces neuroendrocrinological consequences, which lead to cardiovascular and "emotional" syndromes (Gelhorn, 1969). Those forms of neuro-endrocrinological deregulation are engendered in a society in which civilized forms of social con-

[2]The dissociation itself is not the problem, according to Gellhorn, but the lack of rebound to an alternate "relaxed" neuromuscular state. People trained in yoga are able to voluntarily induce dissociation, but since they are able to create voluntary control over emotional states and muscular relaxation, they are not adversely affected by this dissociation.

[3]In order to support his position, Gellhorn cites a variety of animal and human studies. In one experiment, human subjects were exposed to strong emotion-arousing stimuli, (for example, gunshots). It was found that a return of the ergotropic (sympathetic) arousal to control levels was enhanced when the emotional excitement was accompanied by bodily expression (1969: 293).

trol predominate—yet "uncivilized" sources of anxiety, anger, and fear persist.[4]

ARMOR, BREATHING, AND RELAXATION

The erosion of bodily regulation can occur not only on an endocrinological or neurological level but the body can also lose adequate control over its musculature and breathing patterns. The accumulation of muscular tension that Wilhelm Reich called "armor" may make it difficult to release such tension and results in the inhibition of the ability to "let go" or relax. Reich defined armor as a shell that develops to protect the individual from environmental onslaughts. Not only is this armor characterological but it is muscular as well; it is the somatic analogue of the personal stance of constant self-control (Robinson, 1969: 23). This protective shell limits the ability of the person to "experience life from within and without" (Robinson, 1969: 23).

This shell develops through a tension between movement towards a form of physical expression, on the one hand, and the social pressure to inhibit such expression on the other. Armor, as pointed out earlier, is developed through what some Gestalt therapists call retroflection, "a chronic holding back, not letting go which results in unfinished bodily business" (Enright, 1970: 112). Each "brake" on spontaneous bodily expression interferes with the natural pulsation of the organism. For a short duration, such "braking" is not bad, in fact, essential for survival, but when it becomes chronic, the body is no longer able to "let go" (Mann, 1973: 63) and thus

---

[4]In a similar vein, social domination that is experienced as arbitrary and that is coupled with external-internal demands for civilized control over anger and aggression may produce what W. Horsley Gantt called "schizo-kinesis," a radical split between behavioral reactions and the physiological reactions of one's heart. Such a form of bodily deregulation, it has been suggested, might contribute to heart disease (Lynch, 1979: 176).

spontaneous responses to stress such as a muscular "relaxation response" become difficult.

One's manner of breathing may also affect the body's ability to relax. Voluntary, conscious control of breathing is central to Benson's (1979) technique of evoking "the relaxation response," as well as to "prana" (breath) yoga and other forms of meditation. Pressures such as those produced by social control can "deregulate" breathing. Breathing can become shallow due to various socially induced fears such as fear of losing control, of being flooded by intense sensual feelings, or the fear of sanctions for expressing anger. Women characteristically exhibit more shallow breathing patterns than men. Muscular tension as well as "constricted" breathing may not only make relaxation more difficult but also amplify the symptoms of a disease. One example is that the severity of respiratory disorders has been linked to shallow breathing, and not simply to the "objective" degree of lung pathology (Ingber, 1981). Asthmatics have been shown to have a more "irregular" breathing pattern than a matched comparison group (Heim et al., 1968). In subsequent chapters, armoring and other forms of deregulation are viewed as the consequence of situations in which spontaneous bodily expressions such as anger are provoked in response to confrontations with arbitrary authority but where social control measures (and one's survival) demand polite behavior and the constant inhibition of such responses.

Another consequence of the constant arousal of the sympathetic nervous system is the accumulation of muscular tension in the form of "trigger zones." These become areas of "self-sustaining neural activity" that act as a source of tonic activity, which under normal conditions is not experienced as pain (Melzack, 1974: 180). When, however, the person sustains injury or pain from another source, these later traumas may combine or "summate" with the activity of these trigger points which "trigger" chronic persistent pain (Melzack, 1974: 176). The relevance of "trigger zones" and of Reichian "armor" to orthopedic problems, such as chronic low back pain or respiratory problems, becomes clear, since they not only affect the body's ability to relax, but "trigger zones" that accumulate from constant body vigilance may later aggravate symptoms.

BODY BOUNDARIES AND SYMPTOMS

Sidney Jourard suggests that a "firmly" but "flexibly" bounded body image may be indicative of optimal body organization or mind-body integration (Jourard, 1964: 97).[5] Since the body is, as Fisher and Cleveland (1968) put it, our "base of operation," how effectively we operate may depend to some extent on how secure we feel our base is. Fisher and Cleveland were the first researchers to systematically examine the relationship between perception of body boundaries and disease. Their studies suggest that the "firmness" of one's body boundary may be linked to places in the body where we are likely to develop disease.

Fisher and Cleveland (1968) found boundary differences— as measured by "barrier" and "penetration" scores—between those with exterior diseases (i.e., rheumatoid arthritis, which affects the extremities) and those with interior diseases (i.e., colitis).[6] Patients with arthritis were characterized by high

---

[5]I will resist making the finer conceptual distinctions that might be made between body schema, body ego and body image, but instead will opt for the global definition: one's body image is simply one's experience (most often "unconscious"—or unarticulated) of one's body. The content and form of our body image, however, not only reflects how we experience ourselves in general (the ego, one can argue, is inseparable from the body), but at the same time is an "object" to which the ego responds. Still, despite their conceptual problems, "global" definitions are useful to unify and connect a variety of phenomena. (For a review of conceptual difficulties and advantages of the body-image concept, see Shontz, 1969.)

[6]The barrier and penetration scores were devised from Rorschach tests. Calling an inkblot an "armadillo" would be a high barrier response, whereas a response such as "it looks like a gaping wound" would receive a high penetration score. The authors do attempt to test the validity of their measures. In one interesting procedure they correlated physiological measures with barrier scores. Thus persons displaying high barrier scores responded to

barrier and low penetration scores and ulcer patients were characterized by low barrier and high penetration scores.[7] They also used these measures to predict responses to stress. High barrier-score individuals could function under high stress conditions more effectively than those with low barrier scores (Fisher and Cleveland, 1968).

Cassell (1965) also found a relationship between body boundaries and symptom localization. He tested the relationship between body awareness and the parts of the body in which a person would be most likely to experience symptoms of illness. Those whose body awareness was focused on the exterior of their body tended to be more aware of exterior symptoms (e.g., numbness in fingers) when ill, while those whose awareness was directed inwards experienced more interior symptoms (e.g., stomach pains). Nichols and Tursky (1967) found that while anxiety about body image is surprisingly not linked to pain tolerance, definitiveness of body

---

stress with lower heart rates but with higher galvanic skin (g.s.r.) and electromyogram (emg—muscle activity) responses than those identified as "low barrier"; in comparison, persons showing low barrier scores showed increased heart rate and lower g.s.r. and e.m.g. responses. Nonetheless, I am very skeptical about the use of such methods and agree with Shontz (1969) that the validity of such a measure and other configurational measures (like the "draw a person" test) has yet to be definitely proven. Fisher and Cleveland, furthermore, use as data Rorschach responses that do not have clear somatic reference (e.g., "a stone walled fortress") and this casts additional doubt on their procedures (Shontz, 1969: 176). Use of the Rorschach, however, reflects Fisher's conventional Freudian assumptions.

[7]In answer to the objection that their findings were an artifact of the experience of having a disease, or caused by the patient's becoming especially attuned to the affected body areas as a result of particular symptoms, Fisher and Cleveland compared two groups—those that had diseases that were clearly the result of mechanical trauma and those that were "psychosomatic." (This is itself a problematic distinction!) The psychosomatic group differed on barrier scores from the non-psychosomatic group. Fisher and Cleveland, however, point out that the psychosomatic group had experienced the symptoms for a longer time (at least four years!), which casts doubt on the validity of their study (1968: 79–81). Thus, despite their study, the question can still be raised: does the disease affect the nature of the body image or does one's body image shape the form that symptoms will take? Arthritic pain in one's joints would help accentuate a sense of body boundaries, thus leading to a "well-outlined" body image. The differences in body image then could be due to the symptoms of the disease and not the reverse.

image was. Those who had a clear sense of bodily boundaries had a higher tolerance for experimentally induced pain. The authors conclude that the individuals who had a high barrier score perceived the pain stimulus, but body security was not threatened by it; the "low barrier" individual found the shocks very "threatening to the integrity of his body" (Nichols and Tursky, 1967: 108). It might be interesting to study whether pain in various body parts is related to sexist or commoditized values regarding those parts. The question of whether our society in fact encourages uncertainty about, for instance, body boundaries, will be taken up later.

The perceived firmness of body boundaries has also been linked to physiological reactivity. Under stress conditions, the more definite the body image, the higher the increase in exterior body response (muscle activity) and the less the interior response (heart rate). The converse was found for those with a less definite body image (Fisher and Cleveland, 1968: 331). Such connections help to explain the relationship discussed earlier between disease and body boundaries. The authors point out (1968: 361),

> Our frame of reference is based on the idea that any tissue sector is capable to some extent of mirroring the sort of influence associated with the body-image boundary. Indeed, we hypothesize the factors which might lead to the association of the body-image boundary with a new body area would result in a new heightened excitation pattern in that area.

Fisher believes that such a heightened pattern might be the result of a specific body attitude.

> To assert that directing attention to a body part can affect it physiologically is equivalent to stating that the activation of a circumscribed body region can be influenced by the adoption of a specific attitude or set toward it. With increasing frequency it is possible to find studies which indicate that this hypothesis is supportable. (1970: 581)

Physiological arousal engendered by a particular body awareness, they speculate, may eventually continue somewhat independently of other internal bodily communication.

Despite the tentative quality of theory and research in this area, it is an intriguing possibility that we might possess "cognitive maps" of our body that interact with the body's internal communication. The state of that interaction in turn may have subtle effects on our health. What is called body image may be a screen upon which our basic security or insecurity about the world (including the invulnerability of the body as a "base of operations") may be projected. Body image may in turn encourage different styles of bodily attention and hence different patterns of physiological reactivity, which in turn, might be incorporated in our sense of body awareness.

Bakan (1968) has suggested that what he calls "telic decentralization" may be mirrored in one's body image. As both Bakan and Jourard contend, there may be a degree of isomorphism (parallel structure and appearance) between psychological and physiological events. Such an isomorphic relationship would not be surprising considering the intricate connections between mind and body that are now being revealed through research.

Some other interesting theories about the ways psychological and physical states intertwine come from some relatively recent research on pain. Continued "correct" feedback about the condition of our inner environment is essential to our survival. Leprosy victims, deprived of pain sensations, lose their limbs. Feedback that ignores warnings, or perhaps exaggerates them, does not usually threaten our health—but when our body confronts crisis, accurate feedback becomes critical. I have already mentioned that trigger zones, supersensitive areas generating self-firing neural activities, can combine ("summate") with low back pain, and distort by amplification the sensations an individual has of pain. Body armor perhaps also affects body communication by amplifying or deadening somatic awareness. There are cognitive factors, such as our style of attending to bodily sensations, that influence this feedback: social learning and the pressure to live up to certain norms regarding bodily control (e.g., masculine "cool").

Theories such as that of Melzack and Wall regarding pain imply that cognitive factors in themselves, such as degree of attention to body parts or sensations, produce physiological changes that actually modify the physical sensations. For instance, cognitive expectations regarding pain may affect the experience of pain by opening or closing "spinal gate" mechanisms. In their gate control theory of pain (Melzack, 1974), Melzack and Wall argue that pain that does not have an immediate organic source, but persists, is not merely a matter of "suggestion" but of activity in the nervous system that affects the opening and closing of gates located in the dorsal horns of the spinal cord. Pain theorists beginning with Descartes have argued that specific pain stimuli produce an input in which the pain message is sent upward and along the spinal cord to a pain center where an alarm is, in a sense, set off. Melzack contributes to pain theory by arguing that descending messages from the frontal cortex (a "higher" brain center") and the limbic (emotional) system as well as input from other parts of the body all affect the opening and closing of spinal gates that modulate pain messages. Thus, cognitive, emotional, and motivational factors as well as sensory data from other parts of the body may filter perception of pain through their effect on the spinal gates.

Another promising recent contribution to pain theory stems from research which has found natural morphine-like substances produced in the brain. By triggering the substances called endorphins, the body can ameliorate pain sensations. Endorphins, it has also been indicated, can be suppressed or produced by cognitive factors (Bakal, 1979; Feuerstein, 1979). The effect of placebos has been explained as triggering endorphin production by the cognitive expectation of relief. The term "psychosomatic pain" acquires yet another level of meaning here![8]

[8]Medicine does not appear to be geared to studying nonspecific effects on the body. Selye's work is unique in that respect, in that the G.A.S. is a general adaptive response to any number of stimuli. This inattention to nonspecific effects until recently has kept medicine from seriously considering, for instance, how placebos might work. The tendency has been to treat placebo

Another factor relating to pain perception is the feeling of helplessness. Studies have shown that helplessness, which increases both anxiety and depression, may in turn affect our style of attending to pain, and consequently increase our sensitivity to such sensations (Feuerstein and Skjei, 1979). One experiment found that individuals who could administer shocks to themselves and control their intensity had higher tolerance and could endure stronger shocks than those who did not have such controls over their situation (Staub, Tursky and Schwartz, 1971).

If we accept some of the implications of Melzack and Wall's and other research, we have another example of how psychological states can affect the physiological transmission of information about the body. Prolonged anxiety or depression, and possibly learned styles of body awareness, may, over time, disrupt either the gating mechanisms and/or the production of endorphins, thus producing a distorted feedback of bodily information.

How are patterns of body awareness linked to social control and domination? Are there physical consequences to "culturally imposed" inattention or overattention to bodily signals? Holub suggests that cultures may suppress contact with body parts, as in the case of women in our society who may not be in touch with their genital areas. Women, he states, are "raised to be emotionally distant from their vaginas" (1979: 41–42). When the mind is "separated" from an area, there may be decreased sensitivity and hence unawareness of such things as infections. Men, similarly, are taught to ignore pain (Jourard, 1964). One may speculate whether this kind of socialization can lead to alterations in the physiological mechanisms that regulate feedback of bodily sensations.

---

effects as "all in the mind," and yet recent research indicates that placebos actually might trigger chemical reactions in the brain, producing the "morphines within" (such as endorphins) (Sobel, 1980).

I have reviewed *some* possible forms of bodily deregulation and their neurological, endocrinological and muscular infrastructures. When the regulation of body functions is undermined, it can affect health and well-being. This deregulation, I shall argue, can be produced by social control pressures, particularly those that predominate in "modern" social structures.

CHAPTER FOUR

The Individual and Social Control

A QUESTION OF SUSCEPTIBILITY

The issue to be taken up in this chapter is one of susceptibility.[1] Why do individuals differ in their responses to environmental stressors? After all, not everyone "breaks" when their bodies are driven at high speed or placed under other forms of pressure. Suppose it were somehow possible to hold constant differences in biological susceptibility (e.g.,

---

[1] I have already criticized "binary," "either-or" notions of susceptibility. Somatic vulnerability cannot be viewed in terms of the presence or absence of *clinically visible* signs, but is a matter of degree of health and illness. Doyal's criticism of national statistics on morbidity and mortality points to their inherent limitation: "The most fundamental problem, however, is that they refer only to those people who are defined as sick or disabled according to medical criteria, or who have actually died. As a result we are forced to discuss the social distribution of sickness and death rather than being able to assess patterns of health in any more positive sense. It is clear that the absence of death or clinical disease is not in itself synonymous with health, but within the context of the existing techniques of data collection and their underlying philosophy there is no way to solve this conceptual problem." (1981: 58). Thus in the present context, given the "binary" bias of existing research, susceptibility is indicated by the appearance of *clinically* visible symptoms and signs of breakdown.

genetic differences) and take into consideration differences in lifetimes of exposure to physical, biological and chemical stressors. Imagine that one could also hold constant exposure to social and psychological stressors other than those generated by measures of social control.[2] Finally, let us further suppose that we know the complex, synergistic interactions between all these factors.[3] How would one consider what remains—that is, the effect of various social control pressures on an individual as well as the individual's responses to these pressures? This is the question that I wish to examine.

The departure point in any analysis of health and society must be the individual (Moss, 1973). Quantitative methodology and statistical correlations are not totally adequate. To correlate variables such as social class (abstracted and often measured in artificial ways) with incidences of morbidity and mortality (often based on "official data"), is to ignore the dialectical, emergent, historical and contextually bound nature of these relationships. Also such correlations, even if accurate, would account for only a small part of any relationship between health and power, as previously discussed.

A methodological approach that begins with an individual should view a particular susceptibility or its absence as the outcome of an individual's natural history or social career. In holistic medicine, the emphasis is on "each patient's genetic,

[2]It should be obvious that many environmental and self-imposed demands wear down the body. Any kind of situation that is demanding can be seen as stressful, whether it is climbing a dangerous trail for enjoyment or mining coal for wages in a dangerous mine shaft. This "insight" has led people to conclude that stress is an inherent part of life (which it is!) and that we're all under stress (which we are!). But what about "unneeded" stress? And what about the qualitative differences in our responses to negative and positive stress? Some research (Glass, 1977: 183) suggests that not just change itself is harmful stress (as some have claimed)—events must be negative to be linked to disease. It is the uncertainty and helplessness generated by the event that are crucial.

[3]As James House et al. (1979) have indicated, various psychosocial factors may interact synergistically with, for instance, chemical and physical stressors in such a way as to lower immunity to noxious environments, affecting such bodily functions as respiration. The complex interactions that exist between various physical and chemical stressors are barely known, much less those that exist between social and physical-chemical ones.

biological and psychosocial uniqueness as well as the importance of tailoring treatment to meet each individual's needs" (Gordon, 1980: 16). Though statistical data can explain some individual variations in health, the emphasis in holistic medicine is the particular biography, career or life history of the individual. One such "instrument" for recording the unique social, psychological and physical influences on an individual is the "life chart" developed by Adolf Meyer. This chart records not only the disease or illness, its symptoms and the current situation in which they are expressed but also the biography of the patient and the dynamics that brought about the patient's current state (Holmes, 1980: 346). The medical data is organized into an historical framework on the basis of past and present contingencies affecting the illness or disease. The emergent and interrelated features of these contingencies at each phase in an illness or disease's history are charted. The principles that underlie the construction of this "life chart" are not unlike those that are the basis of sociological notions such as "natural history" or "social career."[4] (For the application and early use of the "career" concept to ac-

---

[4]The Holmes and Rahe (1967) social readjustment scale was based on Meyer's life chart. In it, various numbered values were assigned to forty-three life events, according to the degree of readjustment they required. (Thus "death of a spouse" was assigned a value of 100, and a vacation a value of 13). It is interesting to note that subjects in a variety of societies (Japan, Mexico, Denmark and Sweden) ranked items very similarly (Lauer, 1973). Both "negative" and "positive" events are included because they require the individual to adjust to a new situation. Hence the effects of both good and bad events may derive from the powerlessness they induce in an individual. High scores on the scale have proved fairly consistently to be related to the onset of illnesses such as respiratory and heart ailments (Liem, 1981:65–66). These studies indicate that individuals faced with many and/or extreme changes in their lives may be at higher risk of illness in a subsequent six-month period (Rahe and Ransom, 1968). Holmes and Rahe's research is valuable and path-breaking in that it demonstrates a relationship between life events, the powerlessness they induce, and the onset of illness. Such an approach, however, does not deal with the effects of low-level, chronic and diffuse stress. More significantly, the scale takes events out of the context of a person's life. Detailed individual case histories that consider the contexts and the meaning the person assigns to events could be a far richer source of data. It is this "natural history" or "Goffmanesque" career approach that I advocate here.

quiring mental patient status or becoming a marijuana user, see Goffman, 1961; Becker, 1963.) An empirical analysis of the relationship between social control and its effect on an individual's health could employ such a method of organizing its data.

Despite my reservations about quantitative studies, many of them are referred to in this essay in order to illustrate theoretical points. They often effectively point to the relationship between power and health. Yet the intensity and extent, much less the quality, of exposure of individuals to conditions of powerlessness, and the way individuals are taught or pressured to respond to such conditions cannot be measured by crudely quantifying these factors and tabulating them. The methodology that would be needed for qualitative analysis, however, cannot be considered within the scope of this work. It is clear, though, that such a methodology would have to include a history of the various "career contingencies" (Goffman, 1961) that affect the emergence of disease or illness. Such a methodology, while accounting for the individual's unique encounters with these contingencies, would not ignore, as many do, the patterned or "social" nature of such encounters.

As I indicated earlier, the emphasis of most social scientists has been on the way that individuals *respond* to pressures, with a corresponding deemphasis on conditions that generate them. Mechanic (1978A) in reviewing the literature on helplessness and health, concludes that whether or not we in fact control our external environment is a "philosophical issue." What is significant is our subjective response to conditions, our "sense" of helplessness.[5] Thus many social scien-

---

[5]It is true that one's reaction to stressors is related to "*perceived*" locus of control. Thus, one factor that determines how we respond to environmental demands is our perception of whether or not control over our fate lies within our grasp or outside of it. (See, for example, Johnson and Sarason, 1978.) A crucial question, however, concerns the source of our *perception* of control. Though such perception is to some extent a matter of subjective definition, our sense of control most often originates in prior experiences (such as events of childhood). Perceived locus of control, thus, is not just a psychological fact, but is, at least partly, determined by social experience.

tists reduce helplessness to a matter of cognition and not to an artifact of social structure (Waitzkin and Waterman, 1974). This is particularly true of various previously mentioned "cognitive" theories in their analyses of health and society. These fail to see the "dissonance"-producing features of social organizations. Moss, for instance, argues that problems of adjusting to alienating social organizations (such as those found in work settings) do not emanate from the organizations themselves, but from the failure of individuals to learn appropriate means of adjusting to "routine work," "authority," etc. (1973: 163). Lack of work satisfaction becomes the result of personal alienation rather than being caused by the conditions of work itself (1973: 161).[6] Of course, my objections are not meant to invalidate the observations of researchers such as Lazarus (1966), who have shown that environmental stress is mediated by our subjective definition of these stressors. Some of us face the world with confidence, others with fear; some are able to manage without visible damage, others break easily. But many social scientists have used the fact of susceptibility as grounds for emphasizing coping practices[7] or subjective responses to social environments,[8] leaving the environments unexamined. Any stress produced by them is simply a ubiquitous, hence

[6]In Totman's (1979) work, the emphasis on the need of individuals to adjust to oppressive social situations takes a "social Darwinistic" bent. He speculates that perhaps psychosomatic diseases represent an evolutionary mechanism that helps weed out those individuals who cannot adjust to society.

[7]In simplest terms, coping means managing the tension a stressor produces, whereas functioning refers to the ability to engage in various goal-directed instrumental activities (Mechanic, 1978B: 51). (For an excellent reader that highlights the "cognitive appraisal" approach and emphasizes coping, see Monat and Lazarus, 1977.)

[8]An analogous example is the trend in industry to engage in "genetic screening," which is supposed to eliminate from the workplace (and thus discriminates against) those who are perceived as hypersensitive to certain chemicals, among other things. What about "subclinical" effects of noxious chemicals? Must workers be diagnosed as having cancer in order to be considered vulnerable to carcinogens? "Genetic screening" blames the victim and forestalls changes in the work environment which, though "costly," would benefit all workers ("Genetic Tests by Industry Questions Rights of Workers," 1980).

taken-for-granted and inevitable feature of existence. Yet institutional environments vary in their destructiveness. Because of deeply rooted economical and social contradictions, such environments often render individual coping skills ineffective or at best provide a precarious buffer between individuals and the structurally produced events that overwhelm them. The failure to cope often is seen as the failure of an inadequately socialized individual, rather than the outcome of a situation in which coping is more or less impossible (Pearlin and Schoeder, 1978: 18).[9] Furthermore, social institutions favor some coping styles over others: the favored ones work in the interests of institutional domination and may not work for the individual. Males in this society are socialized into adopting and learning as the only solutions, aggressive, competitive, time-obsessed styles of responding to social situations. These styles are compatible with a system that needs competitiveness and uses highly rationalized controls over time and human energy. Such controls are most effective when internalized.

Individuals are thus led to cope with situations (even when they are futile) by adopting styles of overcontrol. As mentioned earlier, this style of coping has been called the Type A personal style which is essentially characterized by making a fetish of self or internal control (Friedman and Rosenman, 1974). Any threat to the loss of control creates anxiety, which in turn further encourages this unworkable and destructive form of coping (Antonovsky, 1979; Glass, 1977).

Qualitatively speaking, control in our society is a "masculine" form of control—aggressive, self-initiated, dominating.

[9]I have already mentioned the middle-class bias of many practitioners of holistic medicine, who recommend styles of coping with stress that are impractical in, for example, blue-collar work situations. Similarly, Harburg and his associates, whose work I discuss later, find that the least destructive response to arbitrary authority is a "reflective" style of coping. Members of the middle class are more likely, however, to be able to adopt this style in their work settings. A reasoning stance, an analytic attitude, a "go talk it out with your boss when he's cooled down" solution, may be more fruitful in middle-class white-collar worlds.

It is a response to a basic insecurity about one's existence—an insecurity veiled by a facade of personal invulnerability. Self-control can become a fetish and "freeze" or inhibit a person, so that letting go (even in situations in which letting go is functional) becomes impossible. This type of internal control is an expression of "bourgeois individualism" that denies the need for supportive social contexts and imposes a stigma on those who either temporarily or permanently display an inability to function or cope, as in the cases of mental patients and alcoholics. In general, the social arrangements that uphold this form of control as the norm create the very conditions that make its exercise difficult.

Women, on the other hand, may well be encouraged by sex-role socialization to adopt coping styles characterized by passivity, dependence—a learned helplessness (Seligman, 1975), a "giving up complex" (Schmale, 1972), leading to a "paralysis of will" (Bakal, 1979: 111, 119–121).[10] Such a paralysis, it has been indicated, affects bodily functioning.

Social norms can encourage us to respond to threats to our sense of self or competence either by "giving up" or by frenetically trying to assert control over the uncontrollable. Helplessness, passive behavior and/or a personal overemphasis on internal control, mastery, etc., are often extreme styles of reacting that prove to be dysfunctional both in their assault on bodily regulation and because they foster a further sense of powerlessness. Social control measures (both internally and externally imposed) therefore generate not only external conditions of powerlessness but also incapacitating coping styles.[11]

[10]In her now "classic" work on women and madness, Chesler (1972) suggests that the label "mental illness" is applied, in fact, to either one of two responses to sex-role socialization. A woman may wholly accept the female role *in extremis* and as a result show a great deal of passivity (as well as depression and other behavioral disturbances) or she may reject traditional role restrictions by acting aggressively (in a "typically male" fashion). In either case, her behavior may be considered a sign of "mental illness."

[11]Statements about psychological modes of coping with stress may also apply to other modes, like smoking and drinking (Guttmacher, 1979). Thus,

It is important to note that, in implying a sharp distinction between "stressor" and one's coping style, a hiatus is created between individual and environment that parallels the artificial distinction often made in psychology between personality and society. These separations tend to obscure the common social origin of both powerless environments and destructive responses. Variations in the person's response to social control measures can be traced to contingencies encountered in the course of the person's "career" within various institutional contexts. Those contingencies come in the form of situations that make a person feel helpless and deprive the person of the ability to cope effectively, which undermines health. When encountered in early childhood, these circumstances are particularly destructive. (Of course, a "good" early childhood is not inoculation against disease, nor does an unhappy one predestine a life of sickness.)

THE FAMILY AS A SOURCE
OF BODILY DEREGULATION

For many persons, childhood is the period of their first struggle for autonomy and validity as a person and also when they feel most overwhelmed and out of control. These experiences and the way people are encouraged to cope with them will not only pattern subsequent social functioning, but will be the first assaults on bodily regulation and lay the groundwork for possible later somatic vulnerability. Since the bulk of this essay draws on illustrative data from adult experiences with work and other settings, a few comments are in order on the relevance of early biographical experiences to social control pressures, their effect on bodily regulation and on later encounters with adult pressures. A number of studies suggest

---

self-destructive habits may not exist apart from stressful situations such as the workplace. They may often be engendered by such situations, not brought in from the "outside" ("Some Job Situations Drive Workers to Drink," 1980: 1).

that those who are made to feel powerless in their family environment and must inhibit their displays of anger and are forced to surrender autonomy to a domineering parent will experience problems with health both in their early and later life history. Thus, asthma has been linked to the struggle against overdominating mothers and appears to have a stronger effect on boys (who are expected to achieve more independence) (Pratt, 1976: 127). Severe asthma in children has also been linked with low self-esteem, compliant behavior, and difficulty in expressing aggression (Panides and Ziller, 1981). Eczema also is said to involve, among other factors in its causation, a similar struggle for independence from an overcontrolling parent figure (Pratt, 1976: 127). Other diseases, such as rheumatoid arthritis, again, are viewed as partly connected to problems with authority and control. Exploratory studies show that early family situations, in which the parents use highly punitive measures, lead to inhibited anger and resentments in children. In adulthood, when those individuals whose families overdominated and inhibited them are confronted with what is perceived as arbitrary and injurious authority, a disease such as rheumatoid arthritis may be precipitated or aggravated (Brown, 1976: 306).

However, such studies are very much exploratory in nature and based on retrospective accounts.[12] They are nonetheless suggestive as to some of the ways in which responses and exposure to early parental control might "summate" or add to the pressures of social control experienced in adult life and how they contribute to assaults on physical functioning. An early childhood of powerlessness, coupled with a socialization that encourages certain "dysfunctional coping responses" (e.g., "giving up" or "withdrawal"), may not only

[12]As Chapters Two and Three made clear, I do not advocate a theory of psychosomatic specificity. Nonetheless, somatic responses to social situations, inducing (or coupled with) somatic vulnerability, may lead to a career of illness in later life. Thus, holding back one's anger has a somatic analogue of holding in one's breath. Should such responses becaome habitual, they might predispose one to respiratory disorders.

affect bodily functioning but can set the stage for decreasing one's ability to manage social control pressures encountered in adult life. The asymmetrical power relationships (e.g., based on age, sex and kinship status) found in the family and the bourgeois values about work (productivity, punctuality, neatness, etc.) that they transmit and reflect help perpetuate relationships found in the social order as a whole. It is likely, therefore, that an individual will encounter similar situations of powerlessness in his or her adult life. Michael Lerner (1979: 2) terms "surplus powerlessness," the reactions to power in the present that are conditioned by powerlessness of the past.

> Over and above the actual powerlessness that people experience by virtue of their lack of power to democratically control what is being brought to them as consumers of products and entertainment, there is surplus powerlessness operating as a psychological legacy that cripples people and makes others believe that they cannot change. (Lerner, 1979: 2)

This is the "psychological baggage" that weighs us down when we try to cope with or function in already difficult situations. This psychological baggage is created by mechanisms of social control that maintain these family relationships and preserve the myths and interests of those in power (i.e., parents). The family is the microcosm in which the larger patriarchal order is reproduced generation after generation. The imposition of controls vary in their harshness and in their effects from family to family. Furthermore, they touch various family members in different ways. Many of those caught in more intense and constricting family politics and those in particularly vulnerable social locations are most prone to being broken.

Family strategies of social control may include placing a person into a "double bind" situation, or imposing the family's definitions on a person, thus invalidating the person's experiences. These strategies are used to sustain family myths ("we are a normal happy family"), or a parental definition of a child ("you were always such a good, quiet girl"). More generally, they are utilized to try to sustain sexist definitions of women as invisible, weak or incompetent. Such invalidation may be resisted by withdrawing or engaging in indirect acts of rebellion, which in turn come to be defined as unprovoked, mysterious and insane by parent, husband or psychiatrist. These gender-related coping responses also lead to other adverse social consequences. Withdrawing, for instance, brings the price of eventually not being able to reestablish control in the world.

Laing and Esterson's (1965) analysis of eleven case histories of "paranoid schizophrenic" women and their sickening family context provides an excellent example of the tangled web of response and counterreaction. The authors of this path-breaking study unfortunately never explicate the connection between the troubles that afflict these eleven women and sexism in the society as a whole, which is institutionalized and perpetuated in individual family politics. These women share the experience of being invalidated as well as overprotected, which in turn atrophied their abilities to cope with the world. All of them were made to feel uncertain about the authenticity of their experiences and insecure about their own competence. Laing and Esterson do not sufficiently emphasize the fact that what these women share is their status as daughters (often the youngest) of lower-middle-class parents who have traditional sexist values. Their common ways of being treated are thus related to their social status as women.

To summarize, the variations in susceptibility derive from differences in an individual's career of exposure to institutionally generated conditions of powerlessness, and the way the individual is socialized or pressured by social situations into adopting coping styles that undermine bodily regulation. The point in an individual's career of the first encounter with situations that foster powerlessness or poor coping styles will be a significant determinant of subsequent coping and biological vulnerability. Also important is the frequency with which such conditions continue to be encountered throughout one's life.

Family life, work life and our experience with public institutions that "service" us are central parts of our lives. Within these institutions can be found relationships of domination based on age, sex, race, ethnicity and class that are sustained by measures of social control. All of us come to be involved, in the course of our lives, in a variety of "class struggles."

> One need not be a Marxist to see, permitting myself some license, the history of all social institutions as one of struggle; husband and wife, parent and child, supervisor and subordinate, priest and parishioner, doctor and patient, teacher and student, officer and soldier, representative and voter, leader and rank and file—all without exception relate to each other in a context of scarcity of resources and power, of different perspectives and interests and motivations. (Antonovsky, 1979: 88)

These "contexts of scarcity," different ideologies, and so forth, lead to social exploitation wherein the more powerful will extract or maintain a relative monopoly over resources or otherwise impose "class" interests. It is for this reason that certain mechanisms of social control will be employed. However, the styles of imposing control, the intensity with which such control is imposed, and our personal responses to it will vary. This partly accounts for the different ways in which we are affected by these struggles.

In the next chapter some forms of control uniquely pervasive in "modern" societies are examined. Following that is a detailed analysis of the pressures generated by these forms of control, the relationships of domination they sustain, and the ways in which these pressures affect our health.

CHAPTER FIVE

Modern Social Control: An Introduction

In the past few centuries, a number of changes have taken place in the styles of social control. So-called "civilized" or modern forms emerged in the course of capitalist development. These included the use of the self as an instrument to motivate production and consumption, the development of refined and pervasive forms of externally imposed disciplinary control, and finally the increased reliance by institutions on informational control (as opposed to the use of sanctions, religious legitimations, and other forms). For many people, the consequence of widespread and increased use of these forms was increased anxiety about one's ability to control one's social environment, about one's existence, and, above all, about one's competence. While none of these forms are historically unique, they have, in being refined, intensified, and extended, taken on a new qualitative texture.

In the sixteenth and seventeenth centuries, characterological changes began to emerge that at first helped to legitimate and stimulate production among the bourgeoisie, but later "filtered" down to sectors of the working class. These changes emphasized the importance of the self (for example, as the locus of responsibility for success and failure), self-control, a disciplined use of time and an assertive way of life. These were the changes that Max Weber, for instance, described in *The Protestant Ethic and the Spirit of Capitalism* (1958).[1] One important dimension of this change is that bourgeois individualism and the emphasis on the freedom and responsibility of the individual became, ironically enough, an instrument of domination. As Fromm (1965: 137) writes, "The 'self' in the interest of which modern man acts is the *social* self, a self which is essentially constituted by the role the individual is supposed to play and which in reality is merely the subjective disguise for the objective social function of man in society." The "self" thus provides the illusion of freedom by being seen as the person's own quality: it becomes the basis of self-imposed social yoking, and is a point within as opposed to external to the person for assigning the blame for failure. The essential feature of such controls thus was its internal nature.

> Thus modern man, instead of having to be forced to work as hard as he does, is driven by the inner compulsion to work which we have attempted to analyze in its psychological significance. Or instead of obeying overt authorities, he has built up an inner authority—conscience and duty—which operate more effectively in controlling him than any external authority would ever do. In other words, *the social character internalizes external necessities and thus harnesses human energy for the task of a given economic and social system.* (Fromm, 1965: 311)

The Type A personal style, described earlier, is the caricatured late twentieth-century heir to these character changes.

[1]The inner compulsion to work, to be responsible for one's fate, is generally seen as characteristic of bourgeois individualism. While this personal style had its origins in the middle classes, it eventually was adopted by segments of the working class. E. P. Thompson, for example, argues that the Methodist religious movement crossed class barriers, bringing a bourgeois style to the proletariat. Thus, exposure to a personal style that embodied the work ethic helped workers develop the inner discipline "essential" to industrial labor. Workers were made into their own slave drivers (1966). (See also Pollard, 1963.)

The changes that first emerged with the development of pre-industrial capitalism and helped pave the way for its industrial form were not only attitudinal in nature. As Elias (1978) points out, these changes also involved an emphasis on the internalized control of bodily expression (e.g., anger, body functions such as sexuality, and elimination). These changes in bodily control are a part of a "civilizing" process, the origins of which Elias traces to the sixteenth century and links to the emergence of the modern nation state. By the eighteenth century, changes could be clearly seen in the way that aggression and other forms of bodily expression were regulated. Using etiquette books as his source material, Elias argues that, with the ascendance of the modern nation state (which was largely the result of bourgeois hegemony), new techniques of control were necessitated as populations had to be pacified and domesticated to an unprecedented degree, while at the same time the state assumed an increasing monopoly over violence. This was accomplished by imposing self-initiated inhibitions on the "spontaneous" display of various kinds of bodily expression (e.g., the show of aggression, toilet habits, etc.).[2] Elias' work (1978) is the sociological analogue of Freud's *Civilization and Its Discontents* (1961). But Elias' analysis is not limited to libidinal impulses, and,

[2]Elias (1978: 258) argues that civilized body control creates a sense of a clearly defined boundary (and one might add, in extreme cases—a barrier) between the individual and the surrounding world: "The firmer, more comprehensive and uniform restraint of the affects characteristic of this civilization shift, together with the increased internal compulsions—that, more implacable than before, prevent all spontaneous impulses from manifesting themselves directly and motorically in action, confront the intervention of control mechanisms. These are what is experienced as the capsule, the invisible wall dividing the 'inner world' of the individual from the 'external world' or in different versions, the subject of cognition from its object, the 'ego' from the other, the 'individual' from 'society'. What is encapsulated are the restrained institutional and affective impulses denied direct access to the motor apparatus. They appear in self-perception as what is hidden from all others and often as the true self, the core of individuality." If we accept this argument, then modern individualism must be viewed not simply as a matter of values, but also as a self-imposed bodily discipline that accentuates the separation between the social world and the private world of an individual.

more significantly, it emphasizes the function of this "civilizing process" as a form of social control that accompanies changes in the relationships of domination.[3] In contrast to Elias, I view the changes he describes in modern manners as serving the cause of social (capitalist) productivity, not merely the need of the modern state for a more pacified, domesticated population.

The changes in social control accompanying the development of the capitalist economic mode of production and its social relationships in the private sphere, included the imposition of a variety of highly refined controls over time and even bodily movements.

> If one of the phenomena of the breakdown of the medieval order was the turbulence that made men freebooters, discoverers, pioneers, breaking away from the tameness of the old ways and the rigor of self-imposed disciplines, the other phenomenon, related to it, but compulsively drawing society into a regimented mould, was the methodical routine of the drill-master and the book-keeper, the soldier and the bureaucrat. These masters of regimentation gained full ascendency in the seventeenth century. The new bourgeoisie, in counting house and shop, reduced life to a careful, uninterrupted routine: so long for business: so long for dinner: so long for pleasure—all carefully measured out, as methodical as the sexual intercourse of Tristram Shandy's father, which coincided, symbolically, with the monthly winding of the clock. Timed payments: timed contracts: timed work: timed meals: from this period nothing was quite free from the stamp of the calendar or the clock. Waste of time became for Protestant religious preachers, like Richard Baxter, one of the most heinous sins. To spend time in mere sociability, or even in sleep, was reprehensible. (Mumford, 1962: 42)

[3]Freud, of course, also saw civilization as a form of control. In his definition of civilization, he distinguished between forces of production and relations of production. Civilization is the means of controlling forces of nature and of regulating the relationships between people (Habermas, 1968: 277). He focused, however, mainly on the psychic consequences of civilization and failed to see its controls as linked to such historically changing relationships of domination as class structure (Schneider, 1975).

Discipline that regulated time use and bodily movement, was imposed not only in the workplace, but in schools and in the newly emergent total institutions (such as those designed for deviants). This fostered the creation of a disciplined readily available work force for the needs of nascent late eighteenth- and nineteenth-century industrial capitalism. As Mumford (1962: 139) cogently portrays, this discipline was not merely tied to work but generated rules of polite and civil "interraction" that had consequences for social production.

> The unison and cooperation produced by these various institutions, from the university to the factory, vastly increased the amount of effective energy in society: for energy is not merely a question of bare physical resources but of their harmonious social application. Habits of politeness, such as the Chinese have cultivated, may be quite as important in increasing efficiency, even measured in crude terms of foot pounds of work performed, as economic methods of utilizing fuel: in society, as in the individual machine, failures in lubrication and transmission may be disastrous.

The "synchronous" operation of even noneconomic institutions such as the school, family, etc., helped to impose a discipline that had, among other things, economic consequences.

Foucault's work (1977) also calls attention to this "new" style of control that clearly emerged by the end of the eighteenth century, with changes in the class structure and in the modes of production. According to him, in earlier times the body was frequently the vehicle through which the sovereign or monarch symbolically displayed his or her power. Public torture, executions and mutilations marked the body with the brute power of authority. By the end of the eighteenth century, the body became, instead, the focal point of a myriad of "technologies of power" that regulated its rhythm and motions and that sought to impose, from without, a technology that would penetrate the soul. The body was increasingly viewed as an instrument to be trained and manipulated, as an object from which energy could be extracted in the most "rational" of ways (Sheridan, 1980: 148). This disciplinary control meant a scheduled existence, a high degree of control over bodily expression. While this expression is controlled in all societies, the new control associated with the ascendance of industrial capitalism is distinct in the attention paid to the individual body, "of exercising upon it a subtle coercion, of obtaining holds upon it at the level of the mechanism itself— movements, gestures, attitudes, rapidity and an infinitesimal power over the active body" (Foucault, 1977: 137). By the nineteenth century, the individual already was subject to a whole set of "'micro penalties' of time: lateness, absence, interruptions of tasks: of activity: inattention, negligence, lack of zeal; of behavior: impoliteness, disobedience; of speech: idle chatter, insolence; of the body: 'incorrect attitudes,' irregular gestures, lack of cleanliness; of sexuality: 'impurity,' 'indecency'" (Foucault, 1977: 178).

By the early part of this century, the industrialized capitalism of the nineteenth century had begun to coalesce into the highly centralized, large-scale "rationalized" systems of production now called monopoly capitalism. These socioeconomic changes brought with them a new refinement in work discipline. The assembly line and scientifically regulated productivity introduced into the workplace even more oppressive control over the rhythm and shape of human motion (Braverman, 1974). This rhythm and motion are not restricted to work settings, but, as I describe later, permeate the private sphere of existence, as do the disciplinary forces that Foucault describes. As Mumford has pointed out, one aspect of living in a "civilized society" is having to "reconcile an external, mechanical time schedule that governs much of our activities with organic, personal, self-controlled time— that subjective time or 'duree' as Bergson called it keeps a different rhythm from the planets and work" (Mumford, 1970: 261). Work time is the prototype of and central influence on collective, "standard" social time; it moves at a pace that is at odds with the individualized "body clocks" of many of those that it dominates. Mumford is aware of this disjuncture, particularly between the mechanical rhythms of clock time and the "pulsating" rhythms of sexuality or play. This split generates "dullness" and "decay" and, he implies, it contributes to bodily deregulation (1962: 70). Similarly, the regulation of motion forces the actor into procrustean body disciplines that do violence to natural rhythms. Time and body discipline in the course of several centuries have been tightened and refined. They are imposed both from inside and outside the body with increasing pervasiveness. As such a state of existence increasingly comes to be taken for granted and as these controls become effectively internalized, these strictures also become less visible as forms of control.

The various historical forms in which time is managed and bodily expression controlled can be seen as relative and contingent on different phases in the development of capitalist modes of production (e.g., industrial capitalism). The economic modes influence more than their immediate economic contexts, and the associated patterns of control come to be used to sustain other power relationships. The relationship between time and body discipline and the external/internal ways in which these are imposed also vary historically with changes in the means of domination—the means of exercising power in the context of economic, political, sexual, racial and ethnic relationships. Yet these historically specific kinds of "time and body" management become taken for granted and viewed as inevitable natural consequences of technology or civilization.

Following the emergence of the "classical" bourgeois social character, a new style emerged around the middle of the twentieth century. Because of the accumulation under monopoly capitalism of large amounts of economic surplus, a consumption-oriented social character emerged. This style, unlike the "classical" one, placed an emphasis on immediate gratification, yet contrived to place the same importance (albeit in a narcissistic way) on the self—a new mutation of bourgeois individualism (Larkin, 1979; Lasch, 1979). Such a personal style has come to be important in encouraging the

absorption of the surplus produced under monopoly capitalism. It coexists uneasily with the traditional style that makes
a fetish of control and achievement, and is characterized by a
"time sickness."[4] The individual is thus placed not only
under an inner compulsion to produce but also to consume,
and, by various pressures (peer, advertising, etc.), is then
encouraged to live up to an identity molded by commodity
standards. These standards include the youthful appearance
and vitality of the body that has become synonymous with
one's "true" self-worth.

> Since youthfulness has been seized and enmassed by capital as
> a sales function, everyone who does not want to be defeated in
> the competitive struggle must undergo a kind of "compul-
> sive" rejuvenation. The face as a mirror of the real experi-
> ences, sufferings, fears and hopes of the human being, as the
> mirror of what his life and aging has really been like, thus
> visibly retreats behind the facial mask, that is, has been
> trimmed to look youthful. This facial mask petrifies into a
> living commodity larvae amidst the rejuvenating commodity
> landscape. (Schneider, 1975: 235)

The unleashed productive forces of monopoly capitalism demand that everyone work harder either producing or consuming commodities (Larkin, 1979). The transformation of
the world into commodities filters into the most personal
and private regions of the self, contributing to a fundamental
insecurity about oneself, and hence to stress.

Another form of invisible control—informational manipulation on both the micro and macro level of social life—

---

[4]This "coexistence" expresses one of the major cultural tensions of contemporary American capitalism. Schneider underscores one form this tension takes: "The contradiction between the actual uniformization of the
consumer and the still-existing consumer and class hierarchy becomes more
acute and thus more and more easily the lever for the creation of an anti-
authoritarian consciousness" (1975: 269). In the 1960s, in fact, such an
"anti-authoritarian consciousness" emerged among middle-class youth in
the form of a "counter-culture" (Foss, 1972). Larkin's (1979) excellent study
of an upper-middle-class suburban high school examines the eclipse in the
1970s of this youth "rebellion" in light of the continued presence of these
contradictions.

has become increasingly prevalent in the twentieth century. The use of direct coercion (e.g., violence, direct sanctions, restraint, and so forth) has been replaced by indirect coercion: the manipulation of information. "The law of force is replaced by the more respectable law of deception"; the "master of social strategy" has become the symbol of our times (Ichheiser, 1970: 137). Advertising, public relations, propaganda, and the social construction of news in the mass media are examples of manipulation on a macro level. In the arena of interpersonal relationships such control ranges from Dale Carnegie courses, the emphasis on one's "projected" image—all significant in the world of white-collar work (Mills, (1956)—to the use of information control on clients and workers in various institutional settings. The monopoly of knowledge in the workplace or in professional settings (teacher-student, doctor-patient, lawyer-client, and so on) and the perpetuation of ignorance among clients and workers become tools in sustaining hegemony.[5] Large-scale, highly rationalized centralized production, particularly under monopoly capitalism in this century, requires not only administration but also the absorption through consumption of the large surplus it creates. The age of advertising which this requirement gave birth to (so aptly described by Ewen, 1976) was paralleled by the rise of informational manipulation in the political sphere and in bureaucratic as well as other work settings.

Numerous white-collar worlds such as those in the service sector were spawned by the need to coordinate complex activities, the need to absorb surplus and create jobs. As Mills (1956) pointed out, this shift towards white-collar jobs (and the "proletarianization" of the old middle class) affected the character of work in that workers increasingly dealt with people and symbols rather than things, and relied increasingly on informational control as a tool. Not only do sales-

[5]Recent movements toward medical self-help clinics, do-it-yourself divorce, small-claims courts, etc., are part of the attempt to demystify this knowledge and reclaim it for the lay person.

men, public relations men and upwardly mobile executives use such tools of control, but so do the participants in the professional bureaucratic relationships that have also pro-liferated in our society. Such relationships allow for a non-coercive control that succeeds through mystification (without resorting to worn-out religious legitimations, for example) and that minimizes potential disruption of hegemony. For example, the activities and commands to which persons are subject are increasingly couched in bureaucratic legal-scientific euphemisms ("servicing a client," "patient man-agement," "we must increase production"). Thus, the poten-tial for "direct" and "open" action is diffused. Increasingly, more spheres of activity rely on the social construction of experience as an instrument of domination (e.g., creating the illusion of consensus). While such instruments of control work in the interests of institutional domination, they pro-duce a significant uncertainty about existence in those who are dominated. Ichheiser, who was a teacher of Erving Goff-man, grasps the consequence of this information control—this manipulation of appearances for the dominated "actor."

> Especially in times like our own, characterized by deep econo-mic insecurities, ideological confusion, fluidity and impene-trability of intricate social processes, by propaganda, advertis-ing, adulteration of goods, the man in the street feels himself far more deeply threatened by those rather "invisible" social dangers than by overt coercion and violence. And he is getting more and more suspicious that these invisible forces by which he is threatened are intentional, and for someone's advantage, manipulated by some band of swindlers "behind the scenes." Consequently   the   swindler—manipulator   behind   the scenes—becomes the main symbol of the predominant fear. (1970: 135)

It may be in part this experience of "civilized" informational control that produces the diffuse anxiety and stress that often are taken by advocates of holistic approaches to be the "natu-ral" consequence of the ambiguities that are inherent in "modern" life.

As indicated earlier, an important feature of modern control is its invisibility and indirectness. It is unique in its imposition through external and internal means of body and time discipline, both in the private and public sphere, in its reliance on informational manipulation, and on the emphasis on the self as an agency of production and consumption. Holistic medicine dimly recognizes the effects on health of such controls but has viewed them as the consequence of "modern time pressures," the armoring effects of "civilization," and the ambiguity of "modern life." Such formulations tend to obscure the fact that these effects flow from various forms of "civilized" social control. The remainder of this essay is a more detailed examination of these forms and their effects on health.

CHAPTER SIX

Personal Invalidation: Building a Sense of Hopelessness and Helplessness

INTRODUCTION

Cockerham (1978: 49) is one of the few sociologists who has recognized the implications of Erving Goffman's works on the self (1959, 1961) for a sociological analysis of health. Attacks on the self, Cockerham argues, can be stressful since the self is regarded as a "sacred object." While it is obvious that, for instance, it has always been painful to be degraded, treated as incompetent and so forth, the way the self is regarded involves historical dimensions. It has, in fact, only recently been conceived of as an "object" much less a "sacred" object.[1] The significance that individuals attach to the self, the way it is conceived, the importance accorded to aspects of the self such as self-control and, above all, the social standards upon which judgments about the self are based, all vary with historical circumstances. As indicated,

---

[1]Burns (1979) points out that the self concept only emerged in psychology in the twentieth century.

the rise of bourgeois individualism helped to encourage an emphasis on the significance of the self, yet forms of social control that denied self-expression or made a feeling of self-worth difficult became increasingly pervasive. For instance, Cockerham (1978: 49) suggests that "stress could be induced when an individual perceives his chosen face or performance in a given situation to be inconsistent with the concept of self he tries to maintain for himself and others in that situation." What he neglects are the social arrangements (apart from the multiple roles of modern life) that increasingly pressure individuals to "choose" situations that demand discrepant performances. An example is found within the ever-expanding service sector, which created more and more jobs that involved the construction of a salable appearance at the cost of one's "authentic" self.[2]

> When white collar people get jobs they sell not only their time and energy but their personalities as well. They sell by the week or month their smiles and their kindly gestures, and they must practice the prompt repression of resentment and aggression. For these ultimate traits are of commercial relevance and required for the more efficient and profitable distribution of goods and services. (Mills, 1956: xvii)

The invalidation of the self is thus built into social situations. A person may be treated or asked to appear as an object, as invisible, or to present a self that is alien, denigrating or hostile to his/her experienced self, all for the purposes of production or efficiency or in order to preserve ideological hegemony (e.g., "we are all one big happy family"). In modern society, given the importance attached to the self and "authenticity," such assaults tend to be experienced as more stressful.

[2] As Fromm says, "If you do not smile, you are judged lacking in a 'pleasing personality' and you need to have a pleasing personality if you want to sell your services whether as a waitress, a salesman or a physician. Only those at the bottom of the social pyramid, who sell nothing but their physical labor, and those at the very top do not need to be particularly pleasant" (1965: 268).

Through family socialization, peer pressure and the mass media, invalidation is effectuated. Individuals are "persuaded" to *believe* that they are incompetent or worthless and simultaneously taught to value competence, control and regard the self as a sort of "sacred object." It is important to remember that invalidation can be stressful even when it is not internalized.[3] What follows is a more detailed examination of some sources and consequences of these types of invalidation.

HOPELESSNESS

As indicated earlier, it is within the family that occur both the first encounters with overwhelming external assaults on the person as well as the initial sources of a weakened sense of self. These attacks continue into adult life, as the individual encounters them as a member of a social class, a racial or ethnic group, a particular sex, and even as a consumer.

Self-invalidation is built into the overall structure of economic and social inequality in which we live ("I'm just a . . ."). The effects of inequality are compounded in American society by remnants of the bourgeois, individualist, "Horatio Alger" myth that suggests all can make it and it's one's own fault if one doesn't. In nineteenth-century America, when the society was more fluid, this myth had some basis in reality; today, in periods of consistent and high unemployment, monopoly conglomerate business, and the decline of the small entrepreneur, it is indeed increasingly a myth (Mills, 1956). Only a comparative few achieve any measure of

[3]The distinction between externally imposed and "self-initiated" (internalized) invalidation being made here is similar to the one made by Schmale (1972), who differentiates between hopelessness and helplessness. The former refers to a condition in which a person perceives the environment as making coping and functioning difficult (in effect, as invalidating), whereas the latter refers to a condition under which blame for failure is directed against the self.

success in this system, while the rest are left behind. Sennett and Cobb (1972: 58) write that "the creation of badges of ability requires the mass to be invisible men." The success ladder is endless and the plastic images of "even greater" success, perfection, and so forth, are all flashed before people as constant reminders of their inadequacies. The media creates superstars and celebrities of the moment. Sennett and Cobb (1972) have illustrated, in their analysis of the "hidden injuries of class" and mobility, that even those who do achieve moderate success pay psychic costs in terms of guilt and resentment of others. They call attention to the link between invalidation as feature of bourgeois social relations and the social control function it serves. The authors argue that "American society benefits when it makes people feel anxious, defeated and self-reproachful for an imperfect ability to command the respect of others" (1972: 153). This benefit accrues from the fact "that society injures human dignity in order to weaken people's abilities to fight against the limits class imposes on freedom" (1972: 153). Since the assaults on the self are not perceived as coming from the conditions of one's powerlessness but instead from within, the doubts about self must be repaired through making sacrifices (e.g., for one's children's college career, thus invalidating many of one's own desires) and by acquiring "badges of ability." The rub here lies in the fact that the use of these sacrifices and "badges of ability" diverts individuals from challenging the limits imposed by a class society, until they have, on their own, gained self-worth in terms of the standards set by that system (1972: 153). Such an achievement is impossible for many people and yet is made into a standard upon which a person's essential being is judged.

Work settings are sources of personal invalidation. Pride and challenge in work are increasingly absent, and autonomy is destroyed under bureaucratic and scientific management. For many, sensitivity to such issues has been deadened so that such elements are no longer sought as working conditions; such physically satisfying conditions are luxuries in a period of increasingly high unemployment, like the present. Under monopoly capitalism work is "deskilled and degraded," and the rhythms and motions of the assembly line, as they invade even white-collar worlds, help to erode self-esteem and job satisfaction (Braverman, 1974; Glenn and Feldberg, 1977). Workers are constantly being reminded of their "childlike" status. Being addressed in terms reserved for children, having to ask one's assembly line supervisor for permission to go to the bathroom, and being reprimanded for overly long bowel evacuations are all examples of these reminders (see Garson, 1977; Terkel, 1974; Pfeffer, 1979). Miklós Haraszti, a poet and sociologist who worked in a Hungarian tractor factory, describes the invalidating consequences of the gulf that exists, even in a "worker's society," between management and those who actually produce (1978: 74–75).

> They [management] constitute the company, not us, and the company is a power over us. They concern themselves with us, while we ourselves are concerned with materials, machines—and above all, with our pay. We work only in the Factory; they work for the Company. They themselves do not decide what their function is, but it amounts to this: registering us, organizing us, protecting us, classifying us, insuring us, keeping us together, keeping us apart, managing us, measuring us, paying us, hiring us, rubber stamping us, instructing us, sanctioning us, blaming us, decorating us, immortalizing us, silencing us, deputizing for us, observing us, examining us, surveilling us, searching us.

Reader's Digest Magazine gives its employees report cards, thus perpetuating the childlike treatment that was a part of school (Garson, 1977: 159). All these conditions help to reinforce a lack of self-esteem, often building on the already flawed self constructed in the family.

Frankenhauser and Gardell (1976: 39) suggest that a social psychological approach to work is based on the assumption "that challenge and pride in work are fundamental ego needs and that any serious threat to these needs will endanger the individual's total well being." Under contemporary capitalist and similar work arrangements, these needs are very much threatened. Much work under capitalism, besides exposing workers to specific biochemical and physical assaults, undermines their sense of self-esteem and job satisfaction. The latter two psychological factors have been linked, for instance, to coronary heart disease (House, 1974).

Ironically enough, the most dramatic forms of invalidation are often directed against those who display physical or mental brokenness. Our laws define disability as the inability to work; we have no use for those who are not productive by these standards and invalidate their essence. Those who are institutionalized, such as the aged in nursing homes, the physically or mentally handicapped, find themselves transformed into materials to be worked upon and are treated as childlike ("We are not wrinkled babies!" states Maggie Kuhn of the Gray Panthers), or as invisible—as socially dead. One of the primary goals of movements such as those of elderly people (e.g., the Gray Panthers) or disabled persons (e.g., the Center for Independent Living in Berkeley, California), and all those deemed obsolete in our society, has been to escape the trap of being treated as if one were invisible or did not exist. Furthermore, the metaphors of social death and invisibility may often turn literal, setting up the conditions for "giving up" on life.

Some of the invalidating consequences of social structure that are also encountered in the workplace and home are amplified by total institutions and social service organizations. Gubrium (1975) provides an excellent example of structurally-produced invalidation in a nursing home. As in other total institutions, top staff, floor staff, and residents-patients inhabit very different social worlds, and the communication that passes between these worlds is "distorted" by hierarchical arrangements. In making room assignments and other decisions, top staff work from a psychologistic picture of the patient-resident (which is constructed with input from the floor staff and very little from the patient). These pictures, truncated from the everyday realities of the patient-resident, are shorn of texture and reconstituted in terms of psychological cliches. They often ignore the residents' or patients' own needs and preferences and substitute instead top staff's psychological stereotypes (e.g., "passive-dependent type"). Such structurally generated consequences not only denigrate the self by ignoring or demeaning it, but they directly affect an individual's ability to cope or function (which in turn becomes a source of self denigration which *in its turn* affects competence). Thus, restricting ground privileges cuts patients off from the outside world, and their skills for dealing with this world increasingly atrophy.

Another contemporary target of invalidation relates to one's perception of one's body. The need of contemporary capitalism to consume the surplus it produces leads to attempts to "colonize" minds not only by getting individuals to consume commodities but by shaping the image they have of their bodies. A person's body image is the physical dimension of the self-concept, and physical self-esteem appears to be related to self-esteem in general (Burns, 1979).

Body image is a fusion of what can only be a limited and mediated sensory experience of our bodies, the responses of others, and how we process this information. Bourgeois culture projects commoditized, idealized images of bodily appearance through the mass media; individuals are invited to compare themselves with these images. For purposes of promoting consumption, commodity producers induce uncertainty about bodily appearance—hence anxiety about body image. Otherwise, commodities, especially those used for bodily transformation (cosmetics, plastic surgery, etc.), would have a limited salability. It is important that the sense of physical self be in constant flux. Fashion requires people who are willing to change not only their dress but also their body. Appearances must be responsive to the manipulation of the "consciousness industry" (i.e., advertising). Capitalism thereby guarantees some of its markets.

In American society, women seem to be particularly affected by body ideals that are determined to a great extent by men's standards, and these are in turn internalized by women. Women's "worth" has long been tied to physical attractiveness. The following bizarre example from MacGregor's (1974: 161) excellent social psychological analysis of plastic surgery illustrates this. "One young woman married less than a year requested breast augmentation to please her husband whose ideal was Raquel Welch. 'My poor husband said he never dated anybody under a 36B until he met me, and, gee I'm a 32A and I think I ought to do something about it.'" Anxiety about the appearance of one's body then might be more of a problem for women than for men. In fact, some studies, such as Schwab and Harmeling's (1968), suggest that women are more concerned about their body image than are men.[4] Other studies conclude that women are more concerned about the relationship of their body to the outside world, evaluate their appearance in terms of external standards and may be more insecure about body areas (Fisher and Cleveland, 1968: 34, 39). Obvious physical disability may affect women's self-concept more than men's (Fisher, 1970: 78). It is not inconceivable that psychosomatic symptoms are more likely to manifest themselves in parts of the body with which one is dissatisfied (Fisher, 1970: 601). Today, with body modification becoming an increasingly salable item, such differences between the sexes as to body anxiety may be disappearing. Men also are increasingly seeking plastic surgery in order to enhance youthfulness and hence job and

[4]Some women are rejecting commoditized or male aesthetic sexual standards and, along with them, anxieties about inappropriate body hair, hair color ("blondes have more fun"), and fears of being unfeminine or asexual because one is muscular or physically "masculine." One woman runner remarks: "I no longer want to surrender to someone else's view of sexuality, because for me, at this point, functionalism and sexuality are fused" (Stone, 1980: 42). She may have resolved her conflicts, but in many women these images may be in conflict and certainly are not "fused." If one regards anorexia nervosa as a disease, then one can see a clear connection between body image and health. This "disease" involves a body-image distortion, often in adolescent girls, who stop or drastically reduce eating to the point of impairing health. Given the fetish about thinness that is "capitalized" on in women, such a bizarre form of coping is not surprising.

sexual marketability. Hair transplants are becoming fairly common. Even holistic "bodywork" may try to impose an "ideal" body type on its clients. One disabled feminist writer documents the subtle hostility among some holistic practitioners towards disabled individuals whose bodies do not and *cannot* fit into this ideal (Lessing, 1981).

What has just been said about women's anxiety about their bodily appearance should not be construed as support for the myth that has to some extent been perpetuated by psychoanalysis (with its notion of "penis envy") that women experience their bodies as being fundamentally inferior to those of men. Despite the apparent contradiction over women's body perceptions, women appear, in fact, more "in touch" with their bodies and more aware of internal signals. According to Fisher (1970: 524) women are slightly more likely than men to have flexible yet clearly delineated body boundaries. Men also seem to be more threatened than women by potential attacks on their body boundaries (Fisher, 1975). It appears, therefore, that while women may experience more stress about the way they look, men are more defensive and less certain about their body as territory and less attuned to internal sensations. Security about one's body seems to be related to security about one's self and the world in which one exists. Given what has been said, one would expect those who have anxiety about bodies to have anxiety about their existence and to be under stress.

In Chapter Three, research was reviewed that postulated a relationship between health and one's sense of body boundaries. What kinds of social factors might contribute to a firm sense of one's body territory, and, conversely, what factors might influence the development of a body image with weak boundaries? To speculate, some of the sources of weakened boundaries may stem from childhood experiences of feeling "owned," of being constrained in physical expression, and of being dominated by parents who continually intrude on the child's "space" and impose time rhythms that are at odds with those of the child's needs (Fisher, 1973). Fisher and

Cleveland summarize some of the features of the "Western way of life" that contribute to weakened body boundaries. (All of those groups they examined were oriented to a "Western way of life," and were middle or upper class).

> The weight of the evidence is in favor of the viewpoint that the Western way of life usually involves early demands for self-regulation of oral, anal, and bladder tensions, the ordering of behavior to mechanistic time schedules, the long-term inhibition of straightforward hostility, the imposition of restraint upon sexual expression until late adolescence, and extended periods of formal schooling designed to inculcate complex patterns of training. The emphasis is upon blocking direct impulse outlets and learning, on the contrary, to secure release through tangential indirect channels. (Fisher and Clevelent, 1968: 284)

Many of these features of "Western civilization" are, in essence, the same ones that I have suggested throughout this work and are related to other forms of bodily deregulation.

Other interconnections can be postulated on the relationship of self-worth and health. There is some evidence that one's self-esteem and sense of self-worth contribute to physical vulnerability and to recovery from illness. As mentioned in an earlier section, researchers such as Schmale (1972), Engel et al. (1969), and Seligman (1975) have argued that there is a strong but not mechanical, one-to-one connection between hopelessness-helplessness and health. A poor sense of self, a lack of ego control, a feeling that one's fate is not in one's hands, a "dispirited"[5] self, have been linked to depression and anxiety (Johnson and Sarason, 1978). All this, in turn, may increase susceptibility to infectious diseases. People with a poor conception of themselves take longer to recover from mononucleosis (Anderson, 1978). Schmale and Iker (1971) even link vulnerability to cancer to a sense of hopelessness. In two groups prone to cervical cancer, they found no other psychological differences between those who

---

[5] A dispirited self feels unimportant, worthless, hopeless, and so forth (Jourard, 1964: 142).

actually got cancer and those who did not, except that the former had higher depression and lower ego strength "scores." (Of course, cancer may cause lowered ego strength and self-esteem!) In another study, tolerance for such symptoms as pain was found to be linked to a lack of self-esteem (Feuerstein and Skjei, 1979).

The biological mechanisms that link depression, low ego strength, and so forth, to a vulnerability to illness are not clearly known. Schmale (1972) suggests that parasympathetic arousal and the accompanying endocrinological changes may be involved. Jourard (1964: 53), in reviewing some of Schmale's research, reiterates his position on the isomorphic parallels between psychological and physiological events and concludes:

> Extrapolating from the many observations and opinions of this sort, the present writer proposed a theory of inspiration-dispiritation. Broadly paraphrased, this theory holds that, when a man finds hope, meaning, purpose and value in his existence, he may be said to be "inspirited," and isomorphic brain events weld the organism into its optimal, anti-entropic mode of organization. "Dispiriting" events, perceptions, beliefs, or modes of life tend to weaken this optimal mode of organization which at once sustains wellness, and mediates the fullest, most effective functioning and behavior, and illness is most likely to flourish then. It is as if the body, when a man is dispirited, suddenly becomes an immensely fertile "garden" in which viruses and germ proliferate like jungle vegetation. In inspirited states, viruses and germs find a man's body a very uncongenial milieu for unbridled growth and multiplication.

Constant and intense social invalidation that is internalized by the person may thus contribute to bodily deregulation.

HELPLESSNESS

Even when invalidation is not internalized, it can still affect the neuromuscular and endocrinological regulation of the body. Long-term, externally imposed control over self-presentation can have sickening consequences. Civilized forms of control often result in bodily armoring, "anger in," and dramaturgical stress—the stress generated by having to maintain social appearances.

Good manners and polite behavior constitute one type of such control. For example, clients of "service organizations," workers, and others who are subject to being "managed" frequently recognize that politeness and good manners are being used to manipulate them.

> Those who have regular contact with the administration hate exaggerated good manners as much as dry, neutral and coldly impersonal behaviour. Maybe workers are wounded when it becomes manifest that they are *pieces*, just as the job they handle is a *piece* in *their* hands. Politeness coming from an adminstrator is identical to my own complete lack of feeling when faced with a job I am about to mill; it is just part of his technical know-how. (Haraszti, 1978: 78)

One of the results of such control is the individual's inability to get a "straight" answer. This will be explored in Chapter VIII. In the present context, it is sufficient to note that politeness and "good manners" are invalidating, even when recognized as a form of manipulation by workers and others.

Encounters with authority, particularly when it is experienced as arbitrary or oppressive, can be stressful, even when the invalidation stemming from encounters with such authority is not internalized. Fanon (1963: 293), the Algerian psychiatrist, dealt with the connections between racial, colonial domination and psychological-physical well-being. In this passage, he establishes a link between responses to Algerian powerlessness in the face of French colonial authority, muscular "armoring," and health.

> This particular form of pathology (a generalized muscular contraction) had already called forth attention before the revolution began. But the doctors described it by portraying it as a congenital stigma of the native, an "original" part of his ner-

vous system where, it was stated, it was possible to find the proof of a predominance of the extra-pyramidal system in the native. The contracture is in fact simply the postural accompaniment to the native's reticence and the expression in muscular form of his rigidity and his refusal with regard to colonial authority.

Such a condition might be especially true for social minorities, who, in the face of the arbitrary exercise of power, are forced to conceal their anger. Funkenstein and associates classified behavioral responses of respondents as either "anger in" or "anger out." Those displaying "anger in" reponses were more likely to blame themselves and not express overt hostility. According to physiological indices, the "anger in" respondents, who were upper-middle-class New Englanders, exhibited more extended physical stress reactions than the "anger out" group (Funkenstein, 1957). The relevance of this finding to encounters of the powerless with social oppression becomes readily apparent. For instance, in a very interesting study by Harburg and his associates (1973), the invalidation of emotional responses among black males was linked to hypertension.[6]

While Harburg et al. acknowledge that the causes of hypertension are not clearly known, they point out there is some evidence (e.g., the anger in/out study by Funkenstein just mentioned) suggesting that "inhibited," "contained," or "restricted" anger may be linked to high blood pressure. Anger responses are greater when the aggression of others is experienced as arbitrary (e.g., housing discrimination, police brutality). When under such conditions the expression of hostility is suppressed, it may lead to high blood pressure. Black American males are among minorities that frequently find themselves in such situations where they are attacked but must restrain their display of hostility. The authors

[6]I suspend disbelief about their methodology, which has at least one flaw—using census tracts to designate populations that are under low or high stress. It is their interpretation of the data that interests me.

found a relationship between suppressed hostility, guilt about expressing hostility (a feature of middle-class "civility"), situations of high stress that were anger producing, and hypertension among black males. They indicate that socialization to suppress hostility may be the highest among "respectable poor," those who are upwardly mobile, upper-class families who stress the importance of politeness, or those who respect and emulate upper-status people.[7] Given that connection between social status, anger, and "civilized" forms of expression, I would suspect that the invalidation of emotional responses in situations in which the attack is perceived as arbitrary, would be most serious among those who are powerless, but who are most subject to internal rather than external mechanisms of social control.[8] It would be those groups who would probably be most sickened.[9]

[7]The families in the study by Laing and Esterson, (1965), cited in Chapter Four were primarily lower middle class.

[8]Other illustrations of the relationship between polite self-control, anger and health can be found in some of the research on the psychosomatic correlates of cancer (though I have stated repeatedly that I am wary of such studies and their dangerous potential for stereotyping and blaming the victim, as well as "desomaticizing" the sources of cancer). Such studies have found, for example, that women with breast cancer are inhibited about expressing aggression and "hide" behind a "facade" of "pleasantness." Patients with prostatic cancer have been found to be "unusually tractable," and "eager to please." Those who do not have good host resistance or responsiveness to treatment and have fewer remissions and shorter terms of survival, were found to be more polite and acquiescent than other cancer patients (Fisher and Cleveland, 1968: chapter 12). Similar observations have been made by Fisher and Cleveland (1968: 55) regarding the expression of anger and hostility among arthritics.

[9]In a later study, Harburg and his associates (1979) again examine different styles of coping with arbitrary authority, finding that styles with social status are related to blood pressure. "Anger out" and "anger in" are "resentful" ways of coping, linked to high blood pressure. The middle class and, interestingly enough, women are more likely to use reflective modes (i.e., thinking out the causes of arbitrariness, going to talk it out with one's boss, etc.). Middle-class people are socialized into anger control at an early age. The use of these modes of coping are not just a function of one's socialization, but of class-bound circumstances that make the use of a given style appropriate or inappropriate. When these authors speak of "inappropriate assertiveness" (e.g., anger out), they neglect to mention that inappropriateness very often is determined by class circumstances. What about "in-

The potentially sickening aspects of invalidation also raise some issues related to the question of the physiological consequences of conformity. For instance, in what was essentially a variation of the classic conformity experiment by Solomon Asch,[10] Costell and Leiderman (1968) attempted to study the effect of conformity pressure on physiological stress. They concluded that there was a "pattern of escalation in the autonomic arousal of independent subjects which tends downward in the direction of the controls" (Costell and Leiderman, 1968: 307). This, they argue, indicates that conformity to group norms may lower the level of autonomic arousal (1968: 308). In effect, they suggest that invalidating one's own response and conforming (at least in behavior) may be a form of coping with group pressure that reduces stress, and that independence involves a prolonged price. The experiment, it should be noted, did not force the "subjects" to invalidate themselves in a "fundamental" or serious way. The authors speculate that, if the yielding minority had been placed into the position of yielding for a longer period, possible feelings of guilt induced by reflecting on one's conformity, might have led to the physiological arousal associated with stress. In any event, one must keep in mind the possibility that invalidating one's own response, in some circumstances, may actually be expedient and preferable to facing social pressure, rather than naively assuming that all forms of invalidation are equally stressful. When, however, people are forced to invalidate themselves continuously and in a way

appropriate reflectiveness"—that is, situations in which such a mode cannot work? In these situations, one cannot go reason with one's boss, etc. The use of this mode may, in the long run, tend to a "talking cure," but does not address the basis for the abuse of power. As I stated earlier, "reflective coping" seems to be bound to class privilege.

[10]In this experiment, subjects were shown two lines and asked to indicate which was longer. When those who were in cahoots with the experimenter stated that one of the lines, in fact the shorter one, was *longer*, many of the subjects followed suit! When the subject had an ally who supported his "deviant" perception, conformity lessened. (See Asch (1952) for more details.)

that assaults their basic self-conception, then the long-range physiological consequences may be adverse.

In a "dramaturgical society" (one in which the manipulation of appearances is a highly complex and self-conscious art), not only are bodily expressions very much controlled, but the very activity of manipulating appearances is, in itself, stressful. Jourard (1964: 144) indicates that whatever feelings or actions are being contained, "it takes energy to suppress behavior." This is particularly true for those who have a socially discreditable self to conceal under the cloak of "normal" appearances. For example, the socially prevalent fear of homosexuality (which is threatening to sexist societies) forces homosexuals into a position of having to conceal their "true" selves in order to survive psychological and social pressure. "Passing" as "straight" may place a person under considerable dramaturgical stress. Apart from the self-hatred that comes from internalizing sexist values, or the repressed anger, there is the constant fear of disclosure:

> Visible lesbians are treated as outcasts or queers. They are ignored, fantasized about, and played with. Lesbians are subject to verbal and physical harassment. Closeted lesbians live in fear of being found out. A lesbian's family may be a source of stress for her as coming out to one's family can often mean risking anger, pain or exile. Drifting apart from one's family may be the result of not coming out. (O'Donnell, 1978: 14)

Closets are the refuge of the powerless, but the use of this refuge brings its price. "Closets are a Health Hazard" was the slogan used by the Bay Area Physicians who marched in a Gay Freedom Day Parade. It should be noted that it is not merely homophobia that can keep people in the closet. There are many social pressures for "appropriate" appearances that demand that one inhibit one's self-presentation: women are forced to hide their competence under the veil of appropriate feminine roles; salespeople must project an ever-smiling facade.

The preceding discussion was meant to be suggestive and not exhaustive, to indicate a relationship between a strong sense of self-worth, an ability to express oneself, social control and health. In the context of societies such as ours in which politeness and other dramaturgical skills become ways of sustaining order and normal appearances, such forms of personal invalidation and their effects are more accentuated.

CHAPTER SEVEN

Killing Time
and Bridling Motion

WORK-TIME AND MOTION

Much has been said, thus far, about the effect of social control on self-worth and self-presentation and the accompanying implications for health. This section examines some of the ways modern social control imposes other limits on functioning, that is, deprives one of the control over the rhythm and motions of one's body. Control over one's movements and the pace at which the individual must function are important resources for competently engaging the world. Domination often deprives people of these resources.

Social control measures that affect the use of time and the shape of human motion are most evident in work situations. Such situations provide the prototype for time and body management seen in other institutional settings, such as the school, which in turn helps prepare individuals for their encounters with the workplace. In the twentieth century, we find a refinement and extension of the domination begun in the nineteenth century, in which the worker was more and more tightly enmeshed in machine-related work (Pollard, 1963). The emergence of the assembly line and associated time and motion studies became a new "rationalized" form of control. The physical movement and rhythm of work came to be regulated in great detail by machines, by highly specific and limiting instructions, as well as the breakdown of work tasks into short, simple, repetitious units of activity (Braverman, 1974). The result of this form of control, used in the pursuit of productivity, was increasingly to place workers (especially those from subordinate minorities) into environments that moved too fast, were deadeningly boring, and that controlled the motions of the body in an unnatural and uncomfortable way.

> The quest for increased productivity in the industrial countries has been most intense in industrial manufacturing. This has enhanced pressures on industrial workers as expressed in ever increasing demands on pace and effective use of working time and in decreasing options for variety, relaxation and social interaction at work. To some extent, the growing demands on the workers emanating from this development tend to be reflected in more frequent dispensary visits, sick leaves and early retirements. Recent cross-sectional studies have shown that poor mental health, psychosomatic disorders and sick leaves are most common among workers holding low-status jobs in industrial manufacturing. (Frankenhauser and Gardell, 1976: 43)

The time pressures of such work environments may be conceptualized in terms of a "load balance": some environments demand too much, too fast; while others demand some degree of involvement yet make too few demands and hence are boring. A load "imbalance" thus involves overload, on the one hand, and underload on the other. These concepts indicate the degree of control one has over the rhythm of one's work experience. "Overload" involves piece-rate work, high demands on attention, and environments that move too fast. "Underload" involves machine controlled work, "standardized motion patterns," "short cycle repetitious operations," and a lack of interaction at work. It is boring and tiring work. Work increasingly involves aspects of both "overload" and "underload" (Frankenhauser and Gardell, 1976: 36).

It should be pointed out here that much psychosomatic research has focused on prolonged "hyperactivity," but underactivity, boredom, or "stimulus underload," which can be just as destructive, have not been as thoroughly researched (Pelletier, 1977: 93). One could speculate on the possibility that "being bored to death" might have some biological truth to it. The following headline, found on a satirical-political postcard, then might not be so farfetched: "Workers Dying of Boredom: A Panel Told."

In a pilot study of sawmill workers it was found that those whose jobs were characterized by a lack of control over their situation (as a consequence of overload and underload) were most likely to have increased catecholamine excretions in their urine. Such excretions of adrenal substances tend to be associated with stress.[1] These workers also reported feeling tired, tense, anxious and ill more frequently than other workers (Frankenhauser and Gardell, 1976: 35). "Data from a pilot study of sawmill workers support the view that machine paced work characterized by short work cycle and lack of control over the work process constitutes a threat to health and well-being."

At times, the pace and lack of control over motion may even produce a "stress epidemic," which is manifested through symptoms of dizziness, nausea, headaches and hallucinatory-like phenomena (Chase, 1980).

> The outbreaks occur most commonly on assembly lines, where each worker performs the same repetitive task over and over—assembling electrical switches, packing fish or

[1]Though this type of a physiological measure of stress is common, the study might be criticized on the basis of the unreliability of catecholamine excretions as physiological indicators of stress. Excretions may vary due to differences in liver metabolism or how rapidly the kidneys excrete them (Moss, 1973: 106). Furthermore, this study, like many others, tends to use only one measure of stress. Few studies on humans utilize multiple measures, and most are conducted in unnatural settings. Innovations such as telemetry, portable devices that allow physiological data to be transmitted over a distance, may change this. Despite these reservations, and others voiced earlier, this study is useful in that it provides illustrations of the generalizations made herein, though not definitive empirical evidence.

punching computer cards, to name a few recent examples. Outbreaks have also been known to occur in schools, which, like assembly lines, are places of highly organized and structured activities in which tension is likely to mount. (*New York Times*, May 29, 1979; p. C1)

The article notes that it is women who are the most susceptible to such outbreaks. Such assembly line hysteria is not really due to sex but to the fact that women end up with the lowest status, industrial manufacturing jobs[2] (*New York Times*, May 29, 1979; p. C2). Hysteria is a "normal" reaction to second-class citizenship and the yokes that accompany it.

In the previous chapter, I dealt with bodily control (e.g., inhibition of anger and aggression) in response to personal invalidation. Work, especially under monopoly capitalism, involves another form of body control—that imposed by work discipline. Work discipline may demand that the body remain stationary for long periods of time, control its physical functions, and move in a mechanical fashion. Whereas the control over bodily expression discussed in earlier sections involves control over the presentation of one's social self, work discipline controls the rhythm and shape of movement for the purpose of enhancing productivity in the workplace.

The pressure of time and restricted motion can be most uncomfortably stressful and physically damaging. A felter (a person who makes luggage linings) in a factory provides an extreme example.

> In forty seconds you have to take the wet felt out of the felter, put the blanket on—a rubber sheeting—to draw out the excess moisture, wait two, three seconds, take the blanket off, pick the wet felt up, balance it on your shoulder—there is no other

[2]A German doctor remarks, as if it were an indisputable truth, "Women are less suited for hard manual labor but more for work that requires quickness, fine co-ordination, agile movements, and a constantly hovering attentiveness. These natural talents of women the economy has used to develop a particular kind of women's work: automated work preparation" (P. Hülsmann as cited in Schneider, 1975: 174). This kind of stereotype conveniently legitimizes exploitation.

way of holding it without tearing it all to pieces, it is wet and will collapse—reach over, get the hose, spray the inside of this copper screen to keep it from plugging, turn around and walk to the hot dry die behind you, take the hot piece of felt with your opposite hand—set it on the floor, this wet thing is still balanced on my shoulder—put the wet piece on the dry die, push this button that lets the dry piece down, inspect the piece we just took off, the hot piece, stack it, count it—when you get a stack of ten, you push it over and start another stack of ten—then go back and put your blanket on the wet piece coming up from the tank . . . and start all over. Forty seconds. (Terkel, 1974: 384–385)

The net result of such conditions is that one *becomes* a machine, but since a machine can tolerate what a human being cannot, the gearing of the body to the rhythm and motions of the machine has destructive somatic effects. Haraszti (1978: 112) offers an excellent phenomenological description of how machine-paced motion can alter one's relationship to bodily sensations.

Even at work, when I have found the rhythm and become one with the machine, thoughts and feelings do not disappear: they change. What disappears is the direct relationship which unites them with me, the identity between me and them. This is very difficult to communicate. The best way I can put it is like this: *I* cease to exist. When the huge side doors of the workshop are opened and the transporters rattle in loaded with material, I *know*—without having a thought as such, I simply *know*—that I am in a freezing draught, but I do not *feel* that I am cold. My back aches, there is a cramp in my fingers, the piece rate is ridiculous: I don't feel or think any of this.

What he describes here is the way in which one's working conditions can put one "out of touch" with one's body.

Research suggests that social class might be related to the degree of sensitivity to illness (Koos, 1954). The reported fact that the lower class shows a decreased sensitivity to such symptoms as backaches, headaches, chronic tiredness, coughing, etc., may be due to social circumstances, including work conditions that deaden awareness of the body's messages. Haraszti's vivid description suggests the possible reason.

The pace and motion of factory work has increasingly been extended to "white collar" work so that the work of key-punch operators like that of many factory workers also has "automaton-like characteristics" (Stellman, 1977: 55).

The extension of such measures of control are a reflection of the tendency towards "proletarianization" of white-collar work. There is a growing deemphasis on skill and on individual control over the work process, and a depersonalization of social relationships, all of which are the result of greater managerial control over work (Glenn and Feldberg, 1977; Garson, 1981).

Even those who are the managers are beginning to experience the alienation of "degraded and deskilled" work, as well as tighter controls. In some work settings, executives are required to use codes which record their activity for the computer at half-hour intervals (Garson, 1981). Garson (1981: 41) concludes: "The movement toward control and standardization is reaching deeper and higher into office and professional work. The drive at all levels—clerks through executives—is for cheaper, more replaceable workers." The efflorescence of computer technology since the 1950s has led to a new and wider range of "work proletarianization" among the white-collar stratum, by introducing highly repetitious, boring machine-paced work into the office. The computer also allows worker supervision to be extended and "individualized." Thus the computer terminal on a supervisor's desk can monitor the number of strokes or lines made by a key-punch operator. The worst of these jobs, of course, go to Black and other minority women (Garson, 1981).

Ironically enough, such work rhythms and controls are increasingly imposed even in those human service organizations that have "broken" human beings as their clients. As this rather bizarre example shows, even welfare and social service (Obers, 1979), as well as health workers,[3] are being "Taylorized":

> Institutional health workers are in a very difficult position. On one side are the business interests who increasingly are trying to organize hospitals like factories. There are now time and motion studies which allow 3 minutes to calm a patient and 4 minutes for an episode of vomiting. Institutional workers are experiencing speed up and lay off so patient care suffers. (Weinstein, 1976)

Clients may also be subject to the effects of the temporal "speed up," in addition to experiencing invalidation in these settings. These factors, according to Antonovsky (1979: 200), affect the "sense of coherence" for all concerned, with special implication for the health of clients. The health problems of clients may be aggravated by an "underload-overload" imbalance and lack of consistency in their experience, and by a lack of participation in matters that affect their fate.[4] Our health care system, in fact, engenders various forms of powerlessness by maintaining a monopoly over knowledge, demanding

[3]The hospital reflects in microcosm the stratification of society as a whole. Blacks, other ethnic and racial minorities, as well as women, are at the bottom of the "pecking order" (Weinstein, 1976: 43). The most exploited, least autonomous medical employees are also the "front line" personnel, under a lot of pressure, who must mediate between the medical world and the patient. Given their own powerlessness, much of their resentment is communicated to and taken out on the patient, or "swallowed." Such a situation is also characteristic of "front line" jobs in other institutions as well (e.g., bank tellers).

[4]Studies such as Volicer's (1977, 1978), for example, find a connection between hospital stress, patient reports of pain, length of hospital stay and physiological indicators of stress, such as blood pressure. In her studies, sources of hospital stress included such forms of powerlessness as the threat of a severe illness, unfamiliar surroundings, financial troubles and isolation from other people, spouse and family. A loss of independence and a lack of information (along with medication problems) emerged as the most important sources of hospital stress. Volicer does not detail the ways in which the bureaucratized-professional healing relationship, carried on in the context of a "total institution" (to use Goffman's (1961) terminology), might produce such stressors.

long waiting periods of its clients (especially the poor), and, in general, assigning them a subordinate role. Some of these circumstances can be linked to the attempts of the healing elite to maintain professional hegemony (Waitzkin and Waterman, 1974).

Tight and complex schedules, long hours and shift work are related to attempts to control time in the interests of productivity but often do so at the expense of the worker's control and quality of life. To argue that our contemporary work hours are long may seem absurd in comparison to, for example, the nineteenth century (when the work week was around seventy hours [Friedmann, 1961: 105]). But this era was atypical and was the period of nascent industrial capitalism and rapid industrialization in which surplus labor value was extracted by lengthening the work day. In earlier societies, such as medieval and other agricultural societies, not only was work more in gear with seasonal rhythms, but the work week was shorter (often around thirty hours a week), and workers frequently labored only fifteen weeks a year (Johnson, 1978; Eyer and Sterling, 1977). In a society such as our, which generates a huge economic surplus, shorter work weeks and longer "breaks" should not be unviable.

Shift work is another kind of work rhythm that came to be "taken for granted" under capitalism but was rarely present in earlier times. More and more people are working in shifts as the investment in machinery becomes greater and the working day is shortened[5] (Levi, 1981: 2). As Lennart Levi (1981, 1978), a Swedish specialist in occupational health, suggests in his review of the literature on shift work, such work often violates the rhythms of the worker's physiological functioning by, for example, not allowing enough time to adjust from one cycle to another (see also Luce, 1971). In one

[5]Though the number of persons in the U.S. full-time labor force working in shifts declined from 7.1 million per week in May 1979 to 7.0 million in May 1980, 11 percent of full-time employees were on late shifts in May 1980 (U.S. Dept. of Labor, 1981).

study, more than one hundred volunteers were exposed to alternating between three days and three nights of continuous work. It was found that diurnal rhythms persisted and the body continued to show daytime variations in performance, fatigue ratings, and physiological indices (e.g., adrenal excretions). Other studies show higher rates of sleep, mood and digestive disorders among shift workers. Levi concludes.

> We found that, although the endocrine system does indeed adapt to the environmental demands induced by shift-work by "stepping on the gas" to keep awake in night-time and "slowing down" in the day to allow for some sleep, the usual one-week cycle does not suffice for a complete adaptation of turning night into day and vice versa. Not even three weeks of continuous night work are enough to cause an inversion of the circadian functions, the original circadian rhythms flatten out but still persist. In addition, switching from habitual day work to three weeks of night work is accompanied by increases in a number of indices of physiological stress and social problems in the workers and in their families. (1978: 8)

Shift work, which, like overtime, may be voluntary on a de jure level (e.g., in terms of a union contract), is often anything but that. Financial pressures or fear of denying a superior's request may make what is "voluntary" in practice a mere farce (Pfeffer, 1979: 87–88). Working overtime or on different shift cycles often intrudes into the personal lives of the worker, eroding leisure time, social support, and, above all, generating exhaustion and a sense of powerlessness.[6]

Experiments allowing employees to control their own time (e.g., "flextime"—allowing workers to choose longer days and shorter weeks or alternative daily schedules) have only been tried in the U.S. by a handful of companies and

---

[6]Some individuals adjust better than others, some prefer certain time cycles, and there are sometimes ways of arranging shifts so that workers have an opportunity to adjust. Most workers, however, do not have sufficient control over these matters and cannot have work schedules compatible with individual needs.

have been primarily restricted to white-collar workers ("Scorecard on Flextime": 27).[7] Even such experiments are strongly limited by overriding fears of declining productivity and managerial control, as opposed to the workers' needs.

The most subtle methods of socially controlling time and dominating the body are found in various "socializing" institutions, such as the school and the family.[8] The *New York Times* article cited earlier indicates that such institutions as school may produce situations that create "assembly line hysteria." This is not surprising since school has the effect of preparing us for inhuman work settings. In Frederick Wiseman's excellent documentary, "High School" (which was filmed in an upper-middle-class school), we find numerous instances in which bodily expression in regimented—in gym, beauty and typing class, marching bands, etc. Many of these forms of body domination can be viewed as preparing students to accept robot-like work in the future.[9] In other instances, such domination affirms and perpetuates gender stereotypes. Some of the educational reformers of the 1960s and 70s addressed themselves to these issues. The open-education movement, for instance, incorporated a physical redesign of classroom space so that children could move about freely within the classroom and corridors. Learning was also seen as an active interactionist process of discovery, not as knowledge imparted from above.

As repeatedly indicated, time pressures need not be exter-

[7]Black workers (both males and females) tend to be overrepresented in late shifts. (U.S. Dept. of Labor, 1981).

[8]I would also include institutions for the mentally ill and "handicapped" in this category. Work therapy for the mentally ill and others may include adjusting them to the assembly line. One doctor in a German state hospital "drills" patients in 4–6 week courses on the workbench. "We instill work discipline and time discipline," he states (as cited in Schneider, 1975: 207). Sheltered workshops thus can be rationalized as being therapeutic as well as being profitable.

[9]Gracey (1972) observes that the fragmentation of time into play and work time, and the structuring of time and space in adult terms, begin in kindergarten. There, children are socialized into learning the student role and eventually their adult roles. This learning, of course, includes appropriate regulation of time, motion, and use of space.

nally imposed, but can derive from an individual's personal style. The Type A personality is an example of this style. This personality is susceptible to coronary disease partly because of what Friedman and Rosenman call the "time sickness" that characterizes it (1974). Thus, one not only can be victimized by environments that move too fast, but can develop an obsessive personal style that results in an even greater overload. Furthermore, this personal style is engendered by norms and patterns of socialization that are peculiar to the constant "future orientation" and restlessness of modern capitalism.

> You see how interesting time is: once you start contemplating it, you discover that everything is connected. That's what Marx found. What is capitalism, after all, but a distortion of time wherein the future exchange value of a commodity takes preference over its immediate value for use? Capital is a bridge in time, a structure built on the frothy base of a fictive future. It is not surprising that the executives who minister to the capitalist system are so vulnerable to the Type A pattern of behavior. (Drummond, 1980: 113).

Among males, as Jourard (1964) has pointed out, the fetish of control (which is also a characteristic of the Type A personality style) itself leads to a variety of consequences that can be seen as sickening. "Time sickness" and emphasis on self-control leads to muscular "armoring."[10] Here the posture of the person is one of constant stressful "fight of flight" response. One might speculate on the price males pay for ever

---

[10]While there are many other factors (including perhaps biological ones), this is one possible explanation for differences between male and female life expectancy. Men die earlier, but women experience more illnesses. It is possible, as Mechanic suggests, that women learn more effective coping skills and ways of caring for themselves, for instance, seeking care or calling in sick, (1978A: 162). One curious way in which control of bodily expression in men may prove unhealthy is through the suppression of crying which may deprive them of the ability to release stress-produced toxins in their tears ("Study Examines Tears of Sorrow," 1980). In any event, men may well pay an ironic price for their kind of power and control. (Nathanson (1975) and Waldron (1976) review other explanations of these differences, in articles that present and critique the available data.)

vigilant self-control (particularly those who are relatively powerless)—which is not sufficiently alleviated by various culturally approved outlets for aggression. The cost would be particularly high in a sexist society in which civilized forms of social control predominate. Jourard (1964) also indicated that, due to their stoic refusal to give in to pain or lose control, men may be led to ignore vital body signals that are signs of serious bodily troubles. (See also Twaddle and Hessler 1977: 105.) As more women "participate" in time-pressured, competitive work situations, they may also tend to adopt this personal style in which "time sickness," competitiveness and an obsession with control predominate, which in turn may be accompanied by a rise in the incidence of illness associated with these factors.

It should be noted that women have historically been used as a source of cheap, "docile" labor, particularly for low-level manufacturing jobs, and more recently, in "pink collar" (e.g., beauticians, waitresses) and other low-status and low-paying service occupations. They were thus subject to the accompanying problems of mechanical and unsatisfying work. In the second half of the nineteenth century, women's participation in wage work declined, but in the twentieth century, due to changes in the economy and the labor needs of two world wars, they entered into the world of wage labor. Although many women returned to "hearth and home" after the Second World War, many others remained in the work force. The split between home vs. work, and work time vs. time needed for child care (in the context of a sexist division of labor in the family) imposed additional pressures on women not experienced by men. In the past three decades women were also faced with increased pressure to consume and to organize the consumption of the family (Doyal, 1981).

WORK TIME, FREE TIME

Externally imposed work rhythms are not limited in their effects to the workplace but spread to the private sphere of existence. Thus, as Friedman (1961) points out, even the character of leisure time is affected by work time. One can regard not just work but other life experiences as being characterized by temporal rhythms of "underload" and "overload" (Antonovsky, 1979: 187). The "load balance" of work life can affect experiences in the private sphere.

This intrusion of work time into the worker's private sphere of life is nicely captured by Pfeffer (1979: 41), a college professor who went to work in a factory for a year:

> Except for shopping at supermarkets that are open all kinds of hours, I could hardly run errands, go see a doctor, or do anything in the community. I found myself unable or unwilling to read papers, though I had been accustomed for years to read the New York *Times* every day. I found myself torn between spending those few precious hours of waking leisure with my son, with my wife or by myself. I found myself, in short and with some important differences no doubt, trying to live with drastically curtailed and compressed free time as millions of American workers have learned to live, snatching moments of personal satisfaction largely from time not sold to others.

Pfeffer, who is used to the "open," free, temporal structure of a college teacher's job, is, by virtue of this contrast, able to offer excellent insights on social control, time and work in his book *Working for Capitalism*.

There is a possibility that not only the rhythms of work may seep into lunch hour, weekends and holidays, but the physiological responses to work stress may also continue long after the day is done. A study by Stroebel (as cited in Luce, 1971: 106) indicated that monkeys continue to show responses to a stressor even when it is absent. Physiological stress responses that lasted several days would appear at the same time of day that the animal had been exposed to the noxious stimuli—even when the stressor was not there. Muller has suggested that the nervous system may retain a memory of traumatic or stress events and continue to react on schedule to its memory alone (as cited in Luce, 1971: 150). Many of us have experienced a mild form of this "carryover" when we are unable to adjust sleep and waking patterns over vacations, and continue to wake up to an inner alarm clock geared to the memories of work time. Levi argues that the inability to unwind is accompanied by the hormonal system's inability to slow down, even in the absence of environmental demands. Thus workers who have been exposed to overtime work show elevations of catecholamines not only during work time but through the next evening as well. The process of "unwinding" may be accompanied by an increase in psychosomatic problems (1981: 53).

The inability to relax in free time may also be the consequence of pressures to frenetically consume. Frenzied consumption kills free time in that time spent consuming, or around commodities, must often be structured in the same way as work time. Not only is time devoted to compulsively "enjoying" commodities, but the activity of consumption requires that commodities be bought, kept and maintained. That means more time to be scheduled and compartmentalized to allow for shopping, getting to sales on time, having things repaired, waxed, shampooed, trimmed and polished. Time spent consuming must, to some extent, be scheduled time, and in this way leisure time becomes regimented too.[11]

> Even days ostensibly outside daily routine, holidays, are occupied with "organized" sports and amusements which, far from being liberating forms of leisure facilitating participation in subjective atemporality, are ritualistic reaffirmations of the daily grind, veritable sermons or morality plays on the value of efficient use of "on" time and the rewards of synchronized cooperation. Indeed, unprogrammed, "idle" or "non-productive," time, eagerly sought and jealously safeguarded in more subjective cultures, is experienced as malaise in machine culture. Its forms are loneliness, boredom, and a feeling of guilt over "wasted" time, i.e., various pathological responses to the now unfamiliar experience of duration unstructured by external determinations. (Dye, 1981: 58–59)

[11]I am not suggesting that people are unable to relax while consuming (e.g., shopping). Many people, however, in fact substitute shopping for other leisure-time pursuits, cultural or recreational. It is the twentieth-century American hobby.

Furthermore, commodities often affect the needs they are supposed to satisfy by, in fact, increasing them. For instance, although household aids and technology have shortened the time spent on certain elements of housework, they have paradoxically also lengthened it: creating more stringent standards of what constitutes a well-kept and clean house ("Cleaner than clean!") and a proliferation of cleaning agents, etc., for every conceivable kind of product and household dirt ("drops that spot," "static free"). A disciplined worker and a disciplined consumer go together hand-in-hand in our society.

The standardization of time and of the work process for purposes of corporate productivity and consumption not only has consequences for the worker's private life but also for persons who do not belong to the labor force. There was a segregation of various spheres of activity that began with the industrial revolution, in which work was increasingly moved out of the home, and which further separated leisure and work. This segregation has made it more difficult for women (and for those who cannot or do not function on "normal" time) to participate in the world of work.

> Parenthood as well as a productive and healthy old age, is incompatible with the modern regime. Because the needs of young children do not adapt well to this work schedule, those women who must leave work for some time to raise families are clearly at a disadvantage. The rising incidence of stress-related chronic diseases seems to indicate that the middle aged who are not thriving and the plight of senior citizens, who are banished into relative poverty, is well-documented. (Stellman, 1977: 202)

Thus, those who cannot work on "standard time" are deprived of the satisfaction and self-esteem that work could bring.[12] As documented years ago, unemployment, on the

---

[12]Several facts should be recognized. First of all, parenthood and working in the home *are* work, though they do not have social recognition as paid, productive, "bona fide" labor. Secondly, as a form of work, they are characterized by recurring boring repetitious tasks, by long hours, often by

other hand, produces "underload," and consequences for health (Jahoda, 1958). Thus, while work debilitates health, unemployment may even be less healthy.

It would be simplistic to assume that the unemployed poor merely have "time on their hands," without examining the quality of this time. As for those poor who are working, they are unable to enjoy the privileges of time-use that go with social class.

> The poor may "have plenty of time," but they had better have time, since a great portion of their time is spent waiting. Their lives are filled with waiting—in hospital emergency rooms and clinics, for unemployment or welfare benefits, for food stamps, in courts, in discount stores, for every service they have claim to. They wait. This waiting can cost them much of their wages. Since many services aren't available in non-working hours, working people paid by the day or hour lose money having to take time off from work for these necessities. But those in managerial positions and upwards can take an hour or half a day for court, dentists, sick children, car repairs, and so on without penalty, or have someone else obtain these services for them. For really important people, as Schwartz points out, servers will bring their services to them. And on those rare occasions when they must wait, as in airports, VIPs will have superior facilities to wait in—like "VIP lounges." Indeed, time is money to all of us, rich or poor. (Henley, 1977: 48)

A newspaper article on stress clinics in the U.S.S.R. ("Special Clinics Give Russians Places to Let Off Steam": 7) indicates that one of the important stressors in Soviet urban life is having to wait in line for shopping, banking, etc. Waits average about eight hours a week or the equivalent of one working day. Not only are these lines contingent on bureaucratic conditions and the absence of competing sources of goods, but also upon one's social status. As Henley points out, the political analysis of time must concern itself with access to

---

socially limiting work conditions, and by many other features that characterize, for example, factory work (Stellman, 1977).

other people's time and control over one's own use of time (1977). Barry Schwartz (1973: 870), in his excellent systematic analysis of the social distribution of power and the use of time, concludes that, "Far from being a coincidental by-product of power, the control of time comes into view as one of its essential properties."

OFF THE TIME TRACK AND LOSING CONTROL

Some people, as they decline in their ability or are unable to function at "top speed," find themselves in surroundings that overwhelm them. In the right context, they might still be able to function well. The disorientation and inability to cope or function is interpreted, for instance, among the aged, as a sign of senility, or, among others, as a sign of mental or social disturbance. Their "states of mind" are viewed as personal and internal in origin, not as responses to environments that move uncomfortably fast or slow. Yet, as a *New York Times* article indicates, when the environment of college students was experimentally speeded up (Kastenbaum, 1971), they also began to show an inability to function and a tendency to become irritable: "In short, those young people began to act "old" and "senile" simply because they found themselves unable to keep pace with the world around them—a situation Dr. Kastenbaum points out that is 'not too bad an analogy to the real life situation of the aged'" (Henig, 1978: 160). This is particularly true of those whose retirement (and even more true of those whose institutionalization) leads them to experience "standard" time as irrelevant; such reactions contribute to the atrophying of their coping skills. (For an excellent discussion of time and "pseudo-senility," see Henig, 1981.) The conclusions above could be extended to those who are chronically ill, and whose social contexts do not allow for activity paced in such a way as to minimize their symptoms (e.g., sufferers of chronic pain, or emphysema patients who suffer from breathlessness) and control the deterioration of their body. The Scandinavian countries have been experimenting with (and there are government subsidies for) part-time work for the disabled, which allows for flexibility in the use of time.

Gioscia (1967), several years ago, suggested an intriguing model of deviance based on Merton's anomie paradigm, but one which used time as a variable. "Achronie" (derived from anomie) was a condition of being out of step with time. A relationship between time and health has been suggested here that would link standard time with one's personal pace and one's health. I would expect "achronie" to be a prominent feature of monopoly capitalist societies, and that particularly affects those who are powerless and lack the resources to control time.

Individuals who cannot "keep up" can become "materials" for both the medical and social service sector. The "need" for such services in turn creates jobs for the middle class. For welfare cases, the unemployed poor, the mentally or chronically ill and other helpless groups, the consequence of such servicing is often to render them even more helpless.

Helplessness among those deemed in need of social services is fostered by a variety of mechanisms, some of which have been previously discussed. One is the very division of labor built into the structure of service institutions that leads to a "short circuiting" of information about, for instance, the client's needs as perceived by the client. Such "bureaucratic invalidation" destroys the person's sense that one can exercise choice or control over movements and environment. This may have sickening consequences (Seligman, 1975). Studies on intra-institutional relocation in nursing homes, for instance, show that involuntary moves may have a detrimental effect on health and even longevity (Seligman, 1975). Similar studies in other places such as work settings might prove interesting.

Staff interests in efficiency, and getting "bed and body work" done, often leads to strategies that limit the mobility and action of patients. The use of drugs, restraining devices (e.g., strapping a patient in a wheelchair), or the insertion of a

catheter tube into a patient defined prematurely as hope-
lessly incontinent, all lead to the atrophying of the ability to
cope and function. The insertion itself can be seen as contributing to, for instance, elderly patients' "senility" (Smithers,
1977). Given alternate social arrangements (such as those in
which clients are used as resources to help each other), such
strategies might become less necessary.

Those who cannot keep up with time, or who are not fully
capable of what Goffman calls "guided doings" or bodily
control, are stigmatized in our society and at the same time
placed in situations that aggravate their loss of control.[13] As
Goffman indicates, one central theme in our humor draws on
the inability to engage in these guided doings" (1974: 38–39).
Jokes about physical handicaps, drunks, social incompetents
and slapstick express our concern with self-control and our
attitudes towards the physically handicapped and others (including the infirm), who are seen as incapable of full tempo-
ral-bodily control.

To summarize, the bodily discipline and control over time
that are increasingly demanded by work situations permeate
not only the public sphere of labor, but the private sphere as
well. Disjunctures between an individual's body rhythm,
pace and movements, and the collective standards of time
and bodily control imposed by the production needs of
monopoly capitalism, have consequences for neuromuscular
and endocrinological regulation and physiological equilibrium. The process of being socialized into accepting these
collective standards and social control pressures of work lead
individuals to disregard and distrust their bodily signals.
Those individuals who cannot tolerate these disjunctures
and pressures are often institutionalized: placed into settings
that further encourage bodily deregulation, with adverse repercussions for their physical and emotional well-being.

[13]The word "handicapped" is purposely omitted here, because "handicapped" is too narrowly defined, often in terms of service-agency classifica-
tions. The stigma referred to, is not limited to those conventionally defined
as handicapped, but is more broadly applied in our culture to anyone who
cannot function with appropriate physical control or gracefulness.

CHAPTER EIGHT

Informational Troubles

In the first chapter, I indicated that most social scientists studying the social psychology of health have been preoccupied with the sickening consequences of cognitive states (e.g., dissonance) and a lack of appropriate social information. I have attempted to demonstrate that, while such factors are important, they are by no means the whole story. Furthermore, most investigators have not highlighted the fact that the informational "troubles" that individuals experience are produced by the social structures in which individuals must cope and function. As was pointed out in Chapter Five, in modern social institutions information control has become the dominant form of social control (both on a macro and micro social level). In this chapter I will show how informational control has become more sophisticated and self-conscious and thus more subtle and invisible.

Informational troubles are generated by the inherent organization of and strategies employed by the various bureaucratized structures that permeate the fabric of modern society. In work settings, production is characterized by a radical split between management and worker, and, on an informational level, between the planning and controlling of production and its execution. Similarly, in other institutional spheres, the gap between professional bureaucrat and client replicates this asymmetrical power relationship: the monopoly over knowledge sustains the gap in order to keep "management's" options open, or to protect it against repercussions such as lawsuits, malpractice suits, walkouts, and other actions. Such monopolization is of concern to the worker and the client, whose security as well as autonomy are affected.

There is a great deal of evidence that suggests that uncertainty about information important to one's security creates physiological consequences in the individual, which may, in the long run, adversely affect the person's health. While rat studies should not be used uncritically as a basis for human policy, Weiss' (1972) research is suggestive. His research findings on rats support the conclusion that coping activity itself is not the only factor affecting stress and susceptibility to disease. Also crucial is some information or feedback as to whether efforts to avoid danger, pain, etc., have been successful. A lack of predictabilty about the consequences of actions that may have painful or distressing results may thus have adverse physiological effects on bodily regulation. Kiritz and Moos (1974), in their review of the literature, point out that environments with "low clarity" produce high blood pressure. What they do not sufficiently highlight is the fact that it is not the encounters with situations of low clarity, per se, that produce significant changes in blood pressure, but ones that are perceived as threatening and involve encounters with authority. Though they mention this fact, they do not seem to recognize its significance, given their individualistic bias. Similar dissonance theories, that focus on disruption, also consider these psychological states in the abstract and fail to take note of the contexts that make dissonance or disruption threatening and/or repressive.

Informational troubles are an essential part of hierarchical structures and are to a great extent generated by the means of social control that sustain "class" hegemony. For those dominated, informational troubles can include the inability to explain the source of one's distress, the failure of one's coping and functioning to provide relevant feedback as to important life prospects, and the lack of access to information that would help one cope with impending events that shape one's life. These forms of existential insecurity are relevant to health, as suggested by "cognitive-information" oriented theorists of health and society such as Moss (1973), Antonovsky (1979) and Totman (1979).

"Informational incongruity" is one additional source of insecurity about one's existence. Although Moss links such incongruity to immunity and recognizes that it can inhere in or be suppressed by what he calls "information networks,"[1] he does not see it as a property of a certain kind of social organization. Social organization, he argues, is not inherently incompatible with the individual's needs (i.e., does not intrinsically generate incongruity). This may be true of social organizations when spoken of in the abstract, but particular concrete ones are inimical to peace of body and mind. Many of monopoly capitalism's organizational forms, for instance, generate such incongruity, for reasons previously mentioned. In bureaucratic settings that accompany modern capitalism, one of the "social functions of ignorance" is to maintain control over clients or workers (Moore and Tumin, 1949). Pfeffer (1979: 103–104) elaborates on this connection between informational and social control in the work place:

> As indicated, the factory worker's subordination and related vulnerability is affected in part by the company's keeping from the workers sufficient advance information about the factors of production and intentions of the company so likely to affect their lives. Perhaps the company is simply unconcerned with informing workers. To conceive of it as a lack of concern, however, is to miss the point. Keeping workers ignorant of such information is not merely convenient for a management that has their more pressing moneymaking concerns. Keeping workers ignorant also helps management control them. Ignorance particularly in the face of economic instability, makes workers insecure, hanging on for information in

[1]Moss conceives of social relationships as consisting exclusively of an exchange of information between the individual and the social environment.

company handouts that consistently come too late for a meaningful response. Management treats information as a part of its private property and uses information to protect its own authoritarian rule.

Workers are seldom told the rationale for establishing production norms (Haraszti, 1978: 61). These norms, of course, structure and affect the quality of the working day. Information about dangers in the work environment is also controlled by management. Tennessee Eastman (a part of Eastman Kodak), a company whose attitude seems to typify much of the chemical industry, does not give its workers, or for that matter local doctors or government agencies, the generic name of the substances to which workers are exposed. These substances are protected as "trade secrets," and only the trade name or a code number is used. Workers often experience symptoms such as nausea, rashes, headaches, etc., and, while they may suspect the substances they work with, they cannot get definitive information from management (Scott, 1974; Berman, 1979). Often their only knowledge as to the effects of these chemicals comes from rumors or indirect indicators such as, for instance, the fact that those working in high-risk areas are asked to "spit in the can" (give specimens for sputum cytologies) or give urine samples (Kingsport Study Group, 1978: 61). A local doctor in Kingsport, the Tennessee Eastman "company town," reports seeing telltale symptoms in many of his worker-patients or hearing accounts of illnesses their co-workers are experiencing. He concludes: "But you never read about this in the paper. The only way you get it is through the grapevine. Some of the grapevine is probably inaccurate, but I have a feeling as a physician that I'm seeing the tip of the iceberg" (Kingsport Study Group, 1978: 60).

Such uncertainty aggravates an individual's sense of powerlessness and existential insecurity. These social control measures often result in an inability to predict and plan one's career or know the sources of one's distress. Sweden and Norway have sought to remedy some of this uncertainty. Norway has legislation requiring workers to be informed about systems used for planning and control, to be given the training to understand such systems, and to be able to influence their design. In Sweden, law requires that workers on all levels be given comprehensive information about working conditions and their hazards (Levi, 1981: 119–120).

The rise of bureaucracies met the need to observe, classify, evaluate, hire and fire, and in general control large groups of people. This rise brought with it the increased importance of the "dossier," as a mediator between management-professional and worker-client. The dossier, whether in the form of a clinic record or personnel file, contains the bureaucratic portrait that often is not accessible to those portrayed in it (or when it is, only through the intercession of another mediator—a consulting doctor or a lawyer).[2] These portraits are composed of entries that evaluate deportment, productivity, etc., and have a significant effect on the career of an individual.[3] While such records legitimate organizational decisions and provide them with a patina of rationality (Garfinkel, 1967), their contents and conclusions may bear little relationship to the reality and needs of those judged by them. Like a student who often does not understand why a particular grade was received, except through some opaque, arcane process known only to the teacher, so mental patients, workers and other dominated groups do not understand the rationale behind firing, hiring, reprimands, denial of parole, denial of tenure, etc. It is this disjucture between institutional logic and an individual's interpretation of reality that is a source of "informational troubles" for the person and may have an effect on the person's health.

"Knowing what hurts you has an inherent curative value," says Selye (1956: 229). Yet doctors, as Waitzkin and Stoeckle (1972) point out, use ambiguity to protect themselves, to

[2]As both the number of mediators, and the social and psychological distance between mediators and the individual increase, so, it could be argued, do the impenetrability and incomprehensibility of their decisions for the individual.

[3]For an excellent analysis of the dossier as a contingency affecting the "moral career of the mental patient," see Goffman, 1961. His analysis might be applied to any number of other institutional contexts, such as the workplace.

leave their treatment options open at the expense of their patient's information security, or to paternalistically protect the patient from unpleasant realities for the patient's "own good." Clarity of information may affect such things as post-operative recovery: patients who were given clear information as to what to expect after surgery required less post-operative medication for pain (Feuerstein and Skjei, 1979).[4] As in the workplace, in the doctor-patient relationship, the "physician's ability to preserve his own power over the patient . . . depends largely on his ability to control the patient's uncertainty" (Waitzkin and Stoeckle, 1972: 187). Such forms of control increasingly characterize the myriad analogous situations in which individuals in our society find themselves.

Not only does the monopolization of knowledge become an instrument of social control, but so does the very style in which information is transmitted. Bureaucratic control—not unlike control in other contexts (for example, the use of tactful and polite "fronts" in a family setting to preserve order)—utilizes potentially ambiguous forms of communication such as bureaucratic language. The strategic use of such language allows those in power the maximum flexibility, the avoidance of definite commitments, and the veiling of the coercive or unpleasant nature of certain decisions. "We must increase our productivity," says a manager to a worker. The "editorial we" is used in this statement to linguistically construct an illusion of community while simultaneously reminding workers of their subordinate status (Haraszti, 1978: 72–73). Lakoff (1975) suggests two elements of polite discourse shared by "legalese," "medicalese" and other bureaucratic styles of communication. The first of these is formality, which gives the appearance of distance of the

---

[4]Studies have found that the medical interview is, on the whole, dominated by the physician's language. Most misunderstandings were shown to occur when patients were unable to understand the doctor's language and the doctor could not or would not understand that of the patient (Hauser, 1981: 110–111).

speaker from what is said. The other element is a certain open-endedness, vagueness, and elusiveness. The use of euphemisms, for instance,

> grants the subject is touchy, but pretends that it is not the matter under discussion. Hence we find academic writing replete with technical terms when it is objectivity and scholarly aloofness that is desired; but we find cocktail party chitchat full of euphemisms, since when we gossip we aren't after remoteness, but we do want to avoid offense by avoiding coming head on with ideas that may not be fully palatable when made explicit. Thus neither the doctor writing on sexual practices in a learned text nor the hostess talking about the doings of her friends to mutual friends might want to use the straight four-letter word that most directly describes the situation. So the doctor expounds: "Copulation may also be enhanced by the use of oleaginous materials," and the hostess gushes, "Selma told me she found Jimmy and Marion doing it with mayonnaise!" (1975: 66–67)

Such styles of communication help soften the discussion of painful issues (such as being fired) without coming right out with what is being said or done but instead "coming out sideways." The textile industry had for years avoided calling byssinosis ("brown lung") a disease, but instead referred to it as a "symptom complex," which it deemed a more scientific label, one which would not "unduly alarm" workers (Stellman and Daum, 1971).

In a relationship of power, the styles of communication just described can serve a number of functions for those who dominate, yet at the same time induce a sense of insecurity and anxiety in those who depend on these decisions.[5] The

---

[5]The matter is quite complex. The same mechanisms of "indirect," "velvet glove" control (such as the use of tact or the professional-bureaucratic equivalent), which frustrate direct action or create ambiguity, also help produce the conditions under which radically different lifestyles can coexist. They may create at least the appearance of tolerance, thus making life more bearable, and they can also be used in creating social-psychological contexts of coexistence (i.e., a "culture of civility"). Such tolerance and civility are an essential part of the anarchist-humanist social-

existential situation is analogous to the experience of the eleven "paranoid schizophrenic" women studied by Laing and Esterson (1965), in which the parents appeared to be saying one thing, but meta-communicated a diametrically opposed meaning which they consciously denied.

The powerlessness of many individuals, particularly of the lower class, is compounded by the fact that they often lack bureaucratic competence and knowledge of bureaucratic etiquette, which is one explanation for the recent proliferation of "advocate" organizations (such as mental patients', welfare clients' and patients' rights groups). Kafka's fiction portrays not only a middle-class nightmare but one familiar to the lower class, who experience bureaucracies as even more arbitrary and inexplicable, becoming a mysterious "them." (It is worth noting that Kafka's writings are drawn from his *employment* as a bureaucrat in an office that handled investigations of workers' claims over industrial accidents.)

In sum, it is not only the monopolization of vital information, but the style in which information is withheld or doled out, that, over long periods of time, create the physiological stress responses that affect bodily regulation and cause disequilibrium.

Thus far, I have limited myself to elaborating some of the ways institutional control of information leads to uncertainty, ambiguity and unpredictability about one's fate. There are other kinds of informational troubles—those that produce anxieties about self-worth and competence. Since troubles generated by social pressures to consume and to be visibly successful were discussed earlier, I only briefly mention them here. As pointed out in Chapter Six, anxieties

---

ism advocated here. However, it is not merely the style of social control that is the problem, but the context of exploitation and domination in which it is employed. The use of these control measures under capitalism, for instance, generates "surplus" emotional repression and informational troubles. Thus, while in bourgeois social relationships such styles are used as a means of domination, these styles also aid in providing the basis for nonviolent relationships between diverse "lifestyles."

about self and self-worth derive from discrepancies between the emphasis a class society such as ours places on success, and the opportunities for realization that our social location make available to us. These anxieties also stem from media images and advertising, which mediate our needs and self-perceptions and create tension between our self knowledge, our wishes, and what we are allowed to become. Commoditized images provide individuals with models that are difficult to live up to—even if one can afford to try. The media portrayal of the mythic image of eternal youth, for instance, as purchaseable and, for that matter, even desirable, pressures us to buy, despite our awareness that the image can never be obtained. This tension, between the "realities" of one's social condition and one's expectations, is a source of anxiety for many people in our society (Antonovsky, 1979). While such tension may be part of the human condition, it is only exacerbated by the fetish of consumption and success in our society.

These forms of control, though they do not produce *acute* stress, may produce chronic, "free floating" stress that diffusely affects the body over a long period of time (Pelletier, 1977: 5 and 157). Such diffuse, long-term effects on the body may not be visible under artificial laboratory conditions which purport to investigate stress factors. Future research would want nonetheless to establish more clearly the empirical connections between social structure, controls specific to that structure, various kinds of information troubles, and the stress these connections produce. In this chapter I have offered some hypotheses about what some of these connections might look like.

CHAPTER NINE

Conclusion:
The Civilized Body

> If other stimuli demand continual attention your own somatic
> sensations never get a chance to re-establish the primacy of
> their own rhythms. "Pay attention, look here, go see where it
> is, sit straight, speak articulately, don't do that," from early on
> this is the way people are drawn away from the basic rhythm
> of their own life. This is called "civilization." There is nothing
> wrong with being civilized, but there is something terribly
> wrong with being overcivilized.
>
> Stanley Kelleman (1981: 8–9)

THE CIVILIZED BODY AND ITS DISCONTENTS

Towards the end of the last century, George Beard (rpt. 1972),
an American physician, wrote on "nervousness" (or what
would be called today psychosomatic illness) as a byproduct
of modern life. Civilization, he argued, was only possible
because of the "necessary evil" of specialization, which man-
dates that "individuals devote exclusive concentration of
mind and muscle to one mode of action." He noted that
modern civilization imposes a tyranny of time. Its demands
for punctuality and its focus on the future create anxiety in

modern man, in contrast to "barbarians" and "savages" who live "happily in the present." Civilization also demands the repression of emotions: among civilized people, "it is not polite to either laugh or cry in public." Beard clearly suffered from an ethnocentric and class bias (he believed that workers do not feel the effects of civilization as intensely, given their "muscle oriented work"). He was also blind to the extent that the "necessary evils" of civilization are determined by the historical context of capitalist exploitation and are not an indispensable prerequisite to maintaining a level of productivity commensurate with a "civilized" and industrial society. Beard *did* perceive some of the psychosomatic consequences of social control that by his time were being felt by the middle class. Beard's perspective anticipated the current viewpoint of most holism and health theorists and shared its limitations.

Like Beard, advocates of holistic approaches have dealt with the effects of civilization in highly individualistic ways and, most importantly, have failed to consider forces such as social control. In this essay, modern civilization has been viewed as a form of social control that can, under certain circumstances (particularly conditions of domination), disempower the body.

A significant part of the holistic world view has been the development of a definition of health that does not limit itself simply to the absence of disease and symptoms, but stresses the importance of the body's control over itself, its rhythms, pace and needs. Holistic medicine emphasizes the importance of the body as healer, defender, mobilizer and regulator of its own resources. With the exception of its politically conscious and radical advocates, most supporters of holistic medicine, however, have not grasped the relationship between social domination and the ability of the body to govern itself.

Many politically radical contemporary advocates of holism were members of the counterculture in the 1960s. The sixties counterculture of middle-class American youth was concerned about self, time, and Puritan restraints on sensual-physical enjoyment and pleasure. The counterculture rejected anxiety about time, emphasized "being here now," and avoided a linear clock notion of time. The inability either to "let go" or to satisfactorily experience one's own (or for that matter, another's) body was seen as a stifling bond to be loosened with the aid of drugs, sexuality, massages, yoga, or encounter groups. A compulsive work ethic was also rejected in favor of a qualitatively richer life.

The focus during this period was on developing the individual's potential. For many, this led, in the seventies, to a narcissistic loss of social consciousness that some critics viewed as a degeneration (for instance, Lasch, 1979). For others, focusing on the individual resulted in a strong humanistic and socially aware activism (such as the feminist movement).

The counterculture's view of the individual was a *qualitatively different* form of bourgeois individualism. Individual competitiveness, aggression, and repressive self-control were devalued in favor of harmony with self, others, body and nature. These new values were nurtured in a "post-scarcity" milieu (Bookchin, 1971), and made middle-class youth increasingly aware of contradictions between existing material and social possibilities, and the anachronistic demands that destroyed the body and the self and that deprived individuals of their control over time. (For an excellent study of counter- or "freak" culture origins, values and development, see Foss, 1972.) It was out of this setting that the more radical holistic world views emerged. The cultural and social changes in the sixties thus helped sharpen and revive, on a wider scale, concerns that have since been echoed in holistic medicine.

The holistic approach offers many positive contributions to the understanding and treatment of disease. Research in psychological medicine has begun to establish endocrinological and other bridges between social pressures and disease. A growing body of evidence points to the limits and even iatrogenic aspects of modern allopathic medicine. Yet holistic awareness—even its more radical variety—needs a sociology to complement its individualistic explanations and therapies. To understand how these pressures of civilization relate to social control and domination, one must go beyond the fuzzy formulations of most holistic medicine and look to sociology.

Unfortunately, most sociologists also have inadequately formulated the connection between society and health, relying on Durkheimian assumptions about the relationship of individual to society.[1] One would do better to turn to the works of thinkers like Karl Marx in order to understand the relationship between civilization, domination and health. In the first volume of *Das Kapital*, Marx (rpt. 1977) gives us one of the earliest empirical formulations of a sociology of work. There he links capitalist control of production (not simply the division of labor) to workers' health. Not only does he depict physical conditions as injurious to health, and the social setting as one that deprives individuals of an opportunity to grow, but he shows how the very pace of the work day and the machine-like motions of boring work violate the rhythms of physiological functioning, atrophy skills and in general drain physical vitality.[2]

[1]Emile Durkheim emphasized the predominance of society over the individual and stressed the importance of collective representations (ideas, values, norms, etc.) as opposed to the material-economic infrastructure of society (e.g., social class). His thinking belongs to the French tradition of sociology, whose conservative influence on contemporary sociological thinking is seen in such theories as functionalism (Nisbet, 1966).

[2]Friedrich Engels' work, written in 1845, on "the condition of the working class in England," also abounds with illustrations of how the work process can literally deform the human body. In the following passage, he describes the effects on the bodies of children and women produced by the activity of carrying coal from the mine: "The first result of such over-exertion is the diversion of vitality to the one-sided development of the muscles, so that those especially of the arms, legs, and back, of the shoulders and chest, which are commonly called into activity in pushing and pulling, attain an uncommonly vigorous development, while all the rest of the body suffers and is atrophied from want of nourishment. More than all else the stature suffers, being stunted and retarded." The destructive effects of socially imposed physical movements on the shape of the body and its health have not to this day been adequately investigated by sociologists.

The division of labor under capitalism is also shown to be crippling because, for instance, it separates mental and physical labor, hence, mind and body. Not only does labor activity "split" the individual, but work discipline stifles and restricts the free expression of mind and body. "Factory work exhausts the nervous system to the uppermost; at the same time, it does away with the many-sided play of the muscles, and confiscates every atom of freedom, both in bodily and in intellectual activity" (Marx, 1977: 548). Marx recognized that every division of labor will have some destructive consequences, but under industrial capitalism, this process is carried to the point where a whole new connection between social environment and health becomes increasingly visible.

> Some crippling of body and mind is inseparable even from the division of labor in society as a whole. However, since manufacture carries this social separation of branches of labor much further, and also, by its peculiar division, attacks the individual at the very roots of his life, it is the first system to provide the materials and the impetus for industrial pathology. (1977: 484)

Marx throughout his life consistently returned to his sociological concept of alienation, outlined in his earlier work (1964). In *Das Kapital*, he concretized it, illustrating its sources in the conditions of work that existed in his time, documenting the connection between increasingly "rationalized" systems of bourgeois control over the means of material production and their destructive effects on the worker's body. In the century since Marx's time, with the ascendancy of an increasingly complex industrial and post-scarcity society, further connections between body-mind and sickening social structures have begun to appear. These connections, like stress-induced physical illness, are most clearly perceived by advocates of holistic medicine.

Conditions under capitalism, from Marx's time to the present, have alienated the worker from self and from inner and outer environment. Marxists who have examined the social sources of illness and disease (e.g., Eyer and Sterling,

1977; Navarro, 1976; Doyal, 1981) have generally confined themselves to the sickening consequences of sustaining the material reproduction of society. In this essay, I have attempted to show how bodily deregulation also emanates from the controls imposed in the service of reproducing (i.e., maintaining) cultural-social and political domination.

There are, of course, many ways social systems like capitalism can generate conditions that sicken. Capitalist arrangements that disrupt work, family and community ties, for instance, create the conditions of social isolation for both a metaphoric and actual "broken heart" (Lynch, 1979).[3] In this essay, I have limited myself to the ways in which social control pressures, in the context of domination, "produce" physical disease, illness and death. Civilized control, in particular, in insuring the cultural, political and material reproduction of relationships of domination, disempowers the body by dividing the self against itself, by creating splits between mind and body, and between body and its external-internal environments.

The relationships between social control and bodily regulation, and bodily regulation and health, are not automatic. Clearly, it is possible to have a well-regulated body, yet succumb to disease or trauma; on the other hand, a deregulated body may escape the ravages of disease. Yet the generalization still stands that a body that is constantly deregulated is more likely to experience more wear and tear, more disease and trauma, and more intense symptoms (more pain, for example) when ill.

Social production of disease and illness, furthermore, often requires decades to manifest itself. Its impact is contingent on an individual's particular career of encountering and coping with the pressures that are the fuel of this socially produced illness. The metaphor of "production" might imply that the process is more mechanical than I, in fact, intend.

---

[3]His book shows that loneliness and social isolation can contribute to heart disease.

This metaphor is meant to highlight the reality of the *somatic* consequences of social control pressures.

The destructive effects of civilized or other forms of control are aggravated by the *degree* and intensity of domination and repression that they must sustain. The requirements of polite behavior become a strain when one finds oneself having to respond with a ready smile to the anger provoked by arbitrary authority. Social domination not only increases the sickening effects of social control, but also imposes a "surplus" (more than is essential for collective well-being) of such controls on individuals. It does not allow for differences in psychological-biological needs and capacities to cope with such pressures. These pressures are particularly sickening when they are imposed at the expense of bodily regulation. Individual health is partly a function of a "fit" between environment and particular individual bodily and psychological rhythm and needs.[4]

The somatic consequences of social control are thus determined partly by how intensely the relationships of domination they support are imposed, but they also derive from the types of control themselves. It would, therefore, be misleading to make a sharp distinction between forms of control and the social structures these forms support. As pointed out earlier, varieties of social control change as social structures change. New kinds of control not only reflect structural changes but, in and of themselves, also *embody* new social relationships. Like technologies used to produce and reproduce the material world, forms of control are not neutral. In their very design, machines can objectify types of social relationships. The present conventional design of the telephone, for instance, objectifies two-way, as opposed to group, communication. Similarly, the technology of the assembly line and mass production embody in a material form the work relationships of capitalism. Engels and other early Marxists

---

[4]Lennart Levi (1981: 2), in his work on occupational stress, emphasizes the importance for health of a good "person-environment fit."

fell into the trap of holding a neutral opinion of the means of production and the industrial technology that made it possible. Engels, for instance, saw those who rejected not just capitalist control of industrial work organization, but organizational forms themselves, as unrealistic anarchists; Lenin, as mentioned in Chapter I, uncritically and eagerly embraced Western technologies for organizing human beings for productive purposes. Yet, while social domination aggravates the pressures of control, the forms of control also incarnate relationships of domination. The counterculture of the 1960s voiced a loss of faith in established technologies and began to conceive of alternatives. Bureaucratic structures, which are technologies for managing human needs, also have since come under attack (Dickson, 1974).

But important questions still must be answered—How can some of the sickening consequences of our social life be minimized? What alternatives might exist to our present social arrangements of which the kinds of social control I have discussed are an integral part?—and these questions will occupy the remainder of this essay.

EMPOWERING THE BODY

Any society that wishes to minimize the destructive effects of social control must allow for flexible uses of time. The "load balance" of environments, and a synchrony of individual and collective rhythms, are important components in physical and mental health. Society should encourage environments and personal styles that do not push individuals beyond their capacities yet at the same time sufficiently challenge and energize them. The technology and attendant productive capacities of contemporary capitalist societies provide the material possibilities for individuals to bring time under control.

Social control also entails restrictions on the body's natural movements and ways. Body discipline—particularly that demanded by the workplace: the control over anger, the stifling of spontaneous bodily impulses to play—has become more refined in not only the way it is externally imposed, but the way it is internalized. This fine-tuning and tight bondage at some point become dysfunctional for the *self-* regulation of the individual's body. Social arrangements should support bodily regulation in such a way as to minimally distort body communication, and not underload or overload the person, so as to cause least upset in physiological homeostasis.

Similarly, individuals must know what they can reasonably expect of their world and must be adequately informed so they can choose and plan. Prolonged ambiguity and unpredictability in the face of threats to one's control over the world disempower the body by not allowing it to relax, by placing it under constant stress, and so on. Informational troubles of this sort are produced by the social fact that those in power have a monopoly over information. This monopoly is increasingly utilized more than other sanctions to sustain hegemony in modern societies. The particular social distribution of knowledge that occurs in social relationships such as worker-manager-employer, patient-nurse-doctor, parent-child, is not simply an inevitable matter of expertise over ignorance. Social changes in this distribution of knowledge would equalize communication and enhance the person's ability to control and predict fate (within reasonable possibilities).

Such a redistribution would mean a restructuring of hierarchical relationships such as "professional" ones. Since in a relatively nonexploitative society, the "social functions of ignorance" would be minimized, the individual could obtain the maximum feasible amount of knowledge, hence prevent the body from having to respond physically and repeatedly to a hostile, unpredictable, impenetrable and alien world.

In a class society, there are systematically generated "put downs"—whether they are taken "seriously" by an individual or suffered in silence. This society emphasizes individual control and the authentic *self,* yet makes a fetish out of commoditized images. Its members are exposed to situations in which authenticity must be repressed in the service of socially expedient appearances, or in the face of the arbitrary exercise of authority. The anger turned inward, the repressed rage are transformed into inhibitions that may have adverse somatic consequences. Thus, a significant part of civilized society is in fact based on "uncivilized" hierarchical arrangements. One would expect that a society in which assaults on the self and self-expression are minimized would thereby encourage bodily self-regulation. A truly civilized body, then, is one which has the greatest possibilities for controlling its inner and outer environment. Such self-determination is more likely in situations where the social pressures to produce and consume, and to sustain appearances are not at odds with a strongly held sense of self, and where such pressures are not aggravated, or unnecessarily applied because of a societal requirement to sustain unneeded forms of domination. In this alternative social vision, environments are geared to bodily needs—not solely to production of material goods. Social arrangements would minimize insults that sap the will to live and obviate the rage that is a reaction to oppression, and makes the response of a civilized body destructive to itself.

In a post-scarcity society a form of socialism (closer to Marx's original and as yet unrealized vision) might evolve that would begin to provide such environments and would encourage healthful responses to the vagaries of life. Many of the social controls intrinsic to contemporary society would be dismantled and banished. In a post-scarcity society, these controls are unneeded: "surplus inequality" has become more intensely felt yet increasingly obsolete. As Sennett and Cobb suggest,

> The fact that the United States has arrived at a condition where so much more can be produced than is needed means this country can also afford to stop the diverse process of

evaluation without threatening survival. We can now afford, if that is the term, to recognize a diversity rather than a hierarchy of talents, that is to do away with shaming; it is no longer necessary, if it ever was, for organizations to make a few individuals into the "best" and treat the rest as an undifferentiated mass. (1972: 261)

Bookchin (1971), in his discussion of post-scarcity anarchism, also emphasizes the need to level hierarchical forms. Above all, the integrity of the self must be preserved and defended in any future revolutions. He sees the notion of the masses as one of the most sinister words in the rhetoric of the right and left. In such rhetoric not only integrity of the self is lost but so is concern for the individual's own particular tempo and capacity to function. Freedom is, as Lois Pratt states (1976: 4), conducive to health.

These social changes must occur in society at large and penetrate the spheres of production, consumption, class, sex and age role relationships in a revolutionary way. This revolution must never ignore human suffering (even that of the class "enemy," not to mention of the "masses") or submerge joy or the self. This, I know, is easier said than done. Social change is not just structural, but involves the "repair" of the self and characterological changes (for example, changes in personal uses of time).

> What those who accept Marx's analysis have seldom admitted is that the character structure of most workers is also at fault. With the introduction of this concept into Marx's framework, workers must be viewed not only as prisoners of their conditions but as prisoners of themselves, of their own character structures which are the product of previous conditions. (Ollman, 1976: 249)

As indicated earlier, personality and society are not distinct entities but merely different sides of the same social coin. The personal styles encouraged under capitalism (like Type A behavior) must change along with the structures they support. Not only do Marxists ignore this aspect of change, but they are threatened by the very prospect of such a change. The fear of such a change is not confined to Marxists. Consider the following comments from a physician cited by Zola (1972), a medical sociologist. This doctor describes a personal style that, in light of present medical knowledge, would make an individual less prone to coronary heart disease. According to him, such a person would be

> an effeminate municipal worker or embalmer completely lacking in physical or mental alertness and without drive, ambition or competitive spirit; who has never attempted to meet a deadline of any kind! A man with poor appetite subsisting on fruits and vegetables laced with corn and whole whale oil, detesting tobacco, spurning ownership of radio, television or motor car, with full head of hair but scrawny and unathletic appearance yet constantly straining his puny muscles by exercise. (G. S. Myers, as cited in Zola, 1972: 502)

Zola, of course, is using this quote to illustrate the dangers of medicalizing life, to the point of trying to "prescribe" a personality conducive to physical health. (One can imagine the value judgments involved in trying to assess what a mentally healthy person would be like!) Nonetheless, why should a lack of aggression or competitiveness be synonymous with a lack of physical or mental alertness? What about the energy and vitality that might be expressed by this person in play or love? What is interesting in this quote are the physician's traditional notions of masculinity and traditional values regarding commodities (a person who spurns a car, etc., *must* be strange!). Most significantly, the physician's revulsion at the prospect of such characterological changes shows the tensions that might emerge between current personal styles and those of a future "liberated" generation.

To try to sketch alternatives to the existing system involves utopian vision. Such vision is a product of the imagination; it cannot anticipate social development or simply be imposed on the future. Furthermore, I cannot do justice or give any texture to such a vision in the narrow confines of this work. For one thing, trying to consider necessary social changes is like pulling a small thread from a sweater only to unravel the whole thing. Changing the conditions under which we produce has repercussions for the technology that we use, which, in turn, requires that we reconsider what we produce; of course, what we produce is related to problems of resources, the distribution of products, and so forth. Nonetheless, a little random speculation cannot hurt.

The center for most people's lives is the working day. In the envisioned human-centered society, the start, the length and the rhythm of the work day would be decided by the individual, within guidelines collectively established by coworkers and in accord with societal needs for goods and services. "Flextime" and job sharing would be the norm. Free time would also be extended; leisure and vacation time would not have to be hoarded and vigorously defended against the encroachment of work. Breaks and time off would be interspersed within the work year. The artificial distinction between free time and work time would become increasingly blurred. Work would hopefully become more sensuous and joyous or at least allow the individual to move around, freeing the body of uncomfortable and mechanical motions. The Chinese style of exercise breaks is one possible model. Physical work space would have to be redesigned to provide for movement. Work that could not be made more comfortable would allow for frequent breaks. The working day would include access to "play space," which would be more effectively integrated with work space, and thus factories might be near tennis courts, parks, and similar facilities. More work could be done in the home or in "homelike" environments. The fragmentation of social space that forces us to separate work and play, or learning and play, would be minimized.

What has been said about work is certainly relevant to those institutions in which young people develop, learn and mature. "Open education" classrooms already have redesigned space to allow for freedom and flexibility in physical movement. Incidentally, the college or university campus that the middle and upper classes have such ready access to, with its open temporal structure, provides a possible model for the workplace of the future. It is true that professors are often self-driven, or driven by production quotas to publish or perish; one can see in classroom design the vestiges of puritan asceticism, and, of course, learning is scheduled according to the needs of college administrations not that of faculty or students. Nonetheless, many professors have long summer vacations, semester breaks, and frequent three-day work weeks. They control the pace and content of their own work, and many of them, as a part of their social-class privilege, can integrate such pleasures as reading and various educational pursuits into their work. It seems to me, one way to reduce the dreariness of the work day facing most people who are not so privileged is to reduce the need for alienating labor and, perhaps, more significantly, share among ourselves the unpleasant chores that remain.

An instructive model was the job-rotation policy found in Chinese hospitals, where (at least in theory) a neurosurgeon did the work of an orderly one day a week. (This practice, I understand, has unfortunately been abandoned.) Clearly an orderly cannot do a neurosurgeon's work, yet this does not preclude a surgeon from learning what it might be like to be an orderly; and it should not be inconceivable for an orderly to know and do more than is encompassed by the narrow confines of current job descriptions. "Job enrichment" would become an important social priority. Job rotations should not be forced on us by the mandate of a distant bureaucratic state authority, but perhaps would be something that future generations would do willingly. In any event, new organizational forms will have to be developed that encourage participation, social empathy for the work and life situations of others, and a healthy "person-environment fit."

Our present social contempt for manual, "dirty," or tedious work might decrease, as individuals are made more aware of how material production is accomplished, and how dependent they are on the everyday efforts of the most "unimportant" workers. The media could be used to educate us (after all, we are presently educated into an ethos of commodity fetishism, materialism, as well as elitist, sexist and ageist values). Part of this education could provide resource information relevant to our lives (for instance, about work conditions). It could also teach respect for work in its manifold forms. Success would be seen in terms of quality of effort and hopefully we would learn that it is not merely scientists, managers or supervisors who hold the world up, but we are all like Atlas in our daily productive efforts.

The tyranny of clock time and of mechanical work that now rules in the name of senseless productivity cannot simply be eliminated by collective fiat; fundamental changes in what is produced and the methods of production entail a reexamination of needs, values and priorities. At present we produce (with horrendous energy waste) many unnecessary and even frivolous products. In fact, the existing economic structure—be it the military or the private sector—thrives on waste and built-in physical and psychological obsolescence. As future societies make collective and democratic informed choices about what they produce, they will also reassess the "how" of production. Because the technology that makes production possible is not "neutral," it is essential to reconsider how science will be applied to production, in a human-centered society. As was pointed out long ago by Mumford (1962), this does not mean a return to an agricultural, hand-icraft stage of economic development—a suggestion that is manifestly absurd—but rather means using science to scale down and reorganize production where feasible, and it means a judicious, restricted use of those technologies (e.g., nuclear) that must, by their very nature, remain large scale. Thus, even though solar energy can be harnessed on large-scale reflectors in the sky (as proposed by large corporations), unlike nuclear energy it can also be captured on small reflectors, which can be manufactured in a small-scale, labor-intensive manner and used by individual houses.[5]

[5]See Dickson (1974) for some salient features of alternative technology, and Mumford's (1962) interesting early analysis of the relationship between machines, social structure and civilization. Mumford's speculations, about possible futures and alternatives to existing technology, agree with mine in

Changing the character of the work day along with our limited and destructive definitions of success would allow for broader social participation; this might decrease the extent to which we transform into human waste those who cannot function in some respect at "full" capacity. The fit between person and environment would be enhanced by respecting the differences among individuals, and the value of their contributions and energies.

Throughout this essay, I have emphasized that sources of invalidation in our society do not merely emanate from the class system but from sexist, racist, ageist and other relationships of domination in our society. The various movements for social change that began with the civil rights movement in the sixties are united in their outrage against treating certain social groups as if they were invisible. I have suggested in this essay that invisibility can be unhealthy. Thus the movements of blacks, the elderly, the disabled, women, gays, and others are healthy reactions to this invisibility, and point the way to the possibility of a truly pluralistic society. The pluralistic "melting pot" so often touted by liberals as a characteristic of our "democratic" society would be transformed from myth to reality: the vast variety of human potentialities would flourish and be nurtured. ("Let a thousand flowers bloom!" in the words of Chairman Mao.) In a society that tolerates and encourages diversity, people would not be as pressured to "closet" or hide their identities or capabilities. "Dramaturgical" stress thus would be lessened.

As the need for consumption for its own sake declines, so would the accompanying need for the mustering of social energies towards "selling" and promotion of these commodities. Since true democracy would be extended to all spheres of life and be based on informed choice, citizens would need

---

some ways (such as his emphasis on the importance of crafts and of environments scaled and designed for human needs, his insistence on the necessity to limit (not stop) technical growth and commodity consumption).

to be educated—not by advertising, propaganda and public relations, but by access to full information about the conditions, hazards and consequences of production and the products offered for consumption. With a well-informed producer and consumer, informational troubles might decrease. Part of this is contingent on a shorter work day, since as the society and issues grow more complex, being a well informed citizen becomes almost a full-time job. Bridging the structural chasm between specialists and "the rest of us" is also an essential part of such changes. Informed worker participation, the restoring of connections between producer and consumer, and structural changes that would reduce the need to manipulate individuals, would all help in changing a "mass" society into a society of free individuals.

As I have suggested, our society "short circuits" the flow of information between various groups. The goal of social change would be to restore this flow of information so that, for instance, those who design machines and those who buy and use them, would communicate, consult and enrich each other's informational resources. The same would be true of relationships between patient and healer.

Characterological change might take generations, so one is reluctant to speculate on what form it might take. It is likely, however, that such change will be nurtured in a number of alternative family patterns. Single-parent families— including those with male heads—gay parents, communal and other living arrangements that have emerged in the past decade offer alternatives to conventional family life that may in the future give both parents and children greater choices and flexibility. These changes would encourage deeper respect for children's developing needs and capacities for autonomy. The exercise of parental authority would be tempered by regard for children's rational powers. Destructive gender stereotypes and the traditional division of labor within the family would be altered; changes along these lines are already apparent in some families. As generational differences are bridged, so would the segregation of adult and children's worlds. (I am not suggesting that generational differences should be eliminated, but that they can be softened.) It has been said that "you can choose your friends but not your relatives." Perhaps in the future this will change, allowing individuals who are not compatible with their children, parents or relatives, to find, more easily than at present, surrogate families or communities, not institutional alternatives. Further, as the pressures produced by job insecurity and commodity fetishism decline, so too might some of the pressures that induce wife beating, child abuse, and other family "pathology." If freedom is indeed conducive to health, then the maximization of a free and open society must begin in the family, where the foundation of our personalities is constructed.

Various characterological changes can be envisioned. Emotional controls necessary for community life would still be self-imposed but in a more "economical" fashion. Without the present stifling of healthy anger and disagreements out of fear of social and economic sanctions, the new social personalities that would emerge over time could combine the ability to be civil and tolerant in the face of social differences with an ability to "let go," to express joy, sensuality and passion. Civilized self-control, as defined in this essay, would not be a fetish with its myriad unhealthy consequences. The destructive psychosomatic consequences of such self-imposed control would be minimized since control would not be coupled with social conditions that breed resentment, anger and envy that cannot be expressed. For instance, individuals could more readily speak their minds in a workplace that they control. The aggression bred by domination would thereby decline as would the schism between behavior and inner emotional states.

Such changes, of course, must await large-scale, root social changes. How such changes will come about—and their "inevitability"—are open questions. Structural revolution presently appears remote, and thus the changes I just sketched are, in that sense, utopian. In the meantime, many people are struggling daily with the issues of coping and humanizing life's battles within the confines of the present social system. It is my strongly held belief that any effort that helps people— even if it is short term—should not be scoffed at as palliative or dismissed as a means of cooptation that interferes with inevitable, historically generated revolution.

Workers' clinics, for instance, such as the one at San Francisco General Hospital, are very useful in helping individuals deal with work stress as well as with the complex legal and political machinery that must be battled and mastered in order to receive compensation or to effect even minimal changes in the workplace. At the San Francisco clinic, workers not only get a medical prescription, but a "political" one as well (Piller, 1981). In Oakland, California, the Institute for Labor and Mental Health offers a counseling program that helps workers and their families cope with stress. The Institute runs various support and consciousness raising groups, works with unions, provides training for shop stewards and support for stress-related grievances. The Center for Worktime Options in San Francisco, which is a part of a growing nationwide network, has a resource file and distributes publications. It counsels employees and works with employers and unions in arranging flextime and job-sharing options. The Center also works with those who are about to retire, on ways in which to continue working on a modified schedule ("phased retirement").

Experiments in industrial democracy, though confined by their capitalist context, provide models for work in the future. The Scandinavian countries are the most progressive of Western capitalist societies in protecting their workers and encouraging worker participation. The Saab-Scania plant and Volvo factories in Sweden are the first car factories to eliminate conveyor belts. Small autonomous groups do the assembly at their own pace, often in their own buildings. Production has been scaled down to a human level with the aid of micro-computers (Levi, 1981; Kahn; 1981). The Swedish unions have long been concerned with assembly line boredom and speed-up, and Swedish occupational health research is among the most comprehensive in the world. Workers participate more fully in decision-making, in reviewing corporate medical records, in deciding on how the health budget will be used, and in vetoing or approving plans for new machines (Levi, 1981). The Scandinavian countries have also tried to diminish sex discrimination in the work place. Though often more effective in theory than in practice, some of their efforts, for instance, to subsidize males who go into traditionally "female" types of work and vice versa, have been innovative. These efforts, however limited, at least indicate new directions for the future.

The support groups for workers, people with chronic pain, disabilities, women and men's groups that are proliferating can help to raise consciousness and alleviate some of the destructive social effects on individuals by providing emotional support, shoring up self-esteem, reducing feelings of invalidation, and heightening political awareness. Similarly, women's health care centers can help to prevent and heal illness, where the medical establishment either fails or is inadequate. Unfortunately, many of these types of endeavors are often dependent on unreliable or politically connected government funding and sometimes even subject to harassment by the medical establishment. The Feminist Women's Health Centers, nontraditional, "participatory clinics" in California, were recently notified that they would not be eligible for family planning funds. These centers have been subject to investigations of fraud and have been the targets of bad publicity in the media. Representatives of the clinics consider these problems as attacks by conservatives who favor the medical establishment and their proponents in the state Department of Health (Schnitger, 1981: 1). Such attacks, I would imagine, are not rare and demonstrate the limits of "small scale" changes.

Nonetheless, one promising social development is deinstitutionalization and deprofessionalization of occupations (see Bookchin, 1971; Illich et al. 1977). This thrust, as Bookchin indicates, may help restore a variety of social relationships, such as mutual support, which are lost in a "mass society." Such deinstitutionalization is, of course, limited by structural considerations, such as the monopoly over healing by a medical elite that has narrowly defined both health and healing. Self-care represents a movement, however limited, to deinstitutionalize.

Healing is generally accomplished within the narrow confines of a professional setting and tends to be separated from prevention and above all from everyday life. More shelters for broken humans, better job conditions, more parks, better public transportation, easier access to all of these appear at first to be unrelated to health but are essential to it. These must be important considerations for a holistic/social medicine that is truly "whole," meaning oriented towards changes of economic and social conditions that are unhealthy. I cannot envision the political regime, drug companies, the medical establishment, or the corporate sector giving such changes their highest priority.

Since "civilized" forms of social control are my emphasis, it is possible to read my work as another attempt to resuscitate the healthy "noble savage" or to try to give substance to an "arcadian" or "Utopian" dream of a "Garden of Eden." But a return to a nonexistent, impossible, bucolic-pastoral past, free of stressors, does not have to be the trade-off for health.

As Dubos (1979: 266–267) tells us, dreams of absolute health are static and frozen while reality is emergent and fluid, and social change is tempered by accident and unpredictability. "Any attempt to shape the world and modify human personality in order to create a self-chosen pattern of life involves many unknown consequences. Human destiny is bound to remain a gamble, because at some unpredictable time and in some unforseeable manner nature will strike back." This observation should not prevent humankind from learning from the past and using the present to realize a better future. As McKeown's critique (1979: 183–184) of Dubos, points out, in the course of history we exchange one set of health problems for another, but this does not mean that no progress has occurred.

No form of social change will ever banish disease or grant immortality. For one thing, the limits of our genetic structure, our biological time clocks, preclude such a possibility. However much we try to minimize stressors in the physical environment, some will always be with us. Similarly, the pressures of social life can never be totally eliminated (and I would agree with Dubos that, perhaps like the physical ones, they should *not* be). Some people, in every type of society, will be broken by a fateful coincidence of events in their social experience. Such qualifications do not preclude new horizons of health that might emerge from social changes that would maximize control for the greatest number of individuals over their internal and external environments. This control would include the individual's reappropriation of his or her body. Women would gain control over their reproductive capacities, we would learn to listen to our bodies, workers would not drive themselves, or be driven, beyond their capacities, and the aged would not be placed into "dispiriting" environments that sap their will to live. In short, such changes would strive to encourage social conditions that empower the body and thus allow it a truly civilized existence.

References

Ahmed, Paul I., and Coelho, George V.
  1979   "Toward a New Definition of Health: An Overview."
          In *Toward a New Definition of Health: Psychosocial
          Dimensions*, ed. Paul I. Ahmed and George V.
          Coelho, pp. 7–22. New York: Plenum Press.
Anderson, Robert A.
  1978   *Stress Power.* New York: Human Sciences Press.
Antonovsky, Anton
  1979   *Health, Stress and Coping.* San Francisco: Jossey-
          Bass.
Asch, Solomon E.
  1952   *Social Psychology.* Englewood Cliffs, N.J.: Prentice-
          Hall.
Bakal, Donald A.
  1979   *Psychology and Medicine.* New York: Springer.
Bakan, David
  1968   *Disease, Pain and Sacrifice.* Chicago: University of
          Chicago Press.
Beard, George M.
  1972   *American Nervousness: Its Causes and Consequences*
          (1881). Reprint. New York: Arno Press.
Becker, Howard
  1963   *Outsiders.* New York: Free Press.
Bellingall, Leigh
  1979   "The Rise of Chronic Diseases in Young People."
          Journal of the Nutritional Academy II (October).
Benson, Herbert
  1979   "The Relaxation Response: Techniques and Clinical
          Applications." In *Ways of Health*, ed. David Sobel,
          pp. 331–351. New York: Harcourt Brace Jovanovich.

Berliner, Howard S., and Salmon, Warren J.
   1979   "The Holistic Health Movement and Scientific Medicine: The Naked and the Dead." *Socialist Review* (Jan.–Feb.): 31–52.
Berman, Daniel
   1979   *Death on the Job: Occupational Health and Safety Struggles in the U.S.* New York: Monthly Review Press.
Bloomfield, Harold H.
   1978   *The Holistic Way to Health and Happiness.* New York: Simon and Schuster.
Bookchin, Murray
   1971   *Post-Scarcity Anarchism.* San Francisco: Ramparts Press.
   1962   *Our Synthetic Environment.* New York: Harper and Row.
Braverman, Harry
   1974   *Labor and Monopoly Capital.* New York: Monthly Review Press.
Brenner, M. Harvey
   1979   "Mortality and the National Economy." *The Lancet* II: 568–573.
Brodeur, Paul
   1973   *Expendable Americans.* New York: Viking Press.
Brown, George W.
   1976   "Social Causes of Disease." In *An Introduction to Medical Sociology*, ed. David Tuckett, pp. 291–333. London: Tavistock Publications.
Burns, R. E.
   1979   *The Self Concept.* New York: Longman.
Cannon, Walter B.
   1968   "Self-Regulation of the Body." In *Modern Systems Research for the Behavioral Scientist*, ed. Walter Buckley, pp. 256–258. Chicago: Aldine.
Cassell, Wilfred A.
   1965   "Body Perception and Sympton Localization." *Psychosomatic Medicine* 27: 171–176.
Chase, Laurie
   1980   "Mass Psychogenic Illness." *Science for the People* 12 (Mar.–April): 18–19.

Chesler, Phyllis
1972   *Women and Madness.* Garden City, N.Y.: Doubleday.
Cockerham, William C.
1978   *Medical Sociology.* Englewood Cliffs, N.J.: Prentice-Hall.
Conrad, Peter, and Kern, Rochelle, eds.
1981   *The Sociology of Health and Illness.* New York: St. Martin's Press.
Conrad, Peter, and Schneider, Joseph W.
1980   *Deviance and Medicalization: From Badness to Sickness.* St. Louis: C. V. Mosby.
Cooper, Richard
1979   "Prosperity—the Capitalist Variety—as a Cause of Death." *International Journal of Health Services* 9: 155–159.
Costell, Ronald M., and Leiderman, Herbert P.
1968   "Psychophysiological Concomitants of Social Stress: The Effects of Conformity Pressure." *Psychosomatic Medicine* 30: 298–310.
Cousins, Norman
1976   "Anatomy of an Illness (as Perceived by the Patient)." *New England Journal of Medicine* 295: 1458–1463.
DeBell, Garrett, ed.
1970   *The Environmental Handbook.* New York: Ballantine.
Dickson, David
1974   *The Politics of Alternate Technology.* New York: Universe Books.
Dingwall, Robert
1976   *Aspects of Illness.* New York: St. Martin's Press.
Doyal, Lesley (with Imogen Pennell)
1981   *The Political Economy of Health.* Boston, Mass.: South End Press.
Dreifus, Claudia, ed.
1978   *Seizing Our Bodies.* New York: Vintage.
Drummond, Hugh
1980   *Doctor Drummond's Spirited Guide to Health Care in a Dying Empire.* New York: Grove Press.

Dubos, Rene
  1979   *Mirage of Health.* New York: Harper and Row.
  1968A   *So Human an Animal.* New York: Charles Scribner's
          Sons.
  1968B   *Man, Medicine and Environment.* Middlesex, Eng-
          land: Penguin.
Dye, James W.
  1981   "Man a Machine: A Philosophical Critique." *The
          Journal of Biological Experience: Studies in the Life
          of the Body* 3 (Mar.): 44–60.
Eckholm, Eric P.
  1977   *The Picture of Health: Environmental Sources of Dis-
          ease.* New York: W. W. Norton.
Elias, Norbert
  1978   *The Civilizing Process.* Vol. 1. New York: Urizen
          Books.
Engel, George
  1969   *Psychological Development in Health and Disease.*
          Philadelphia: W. B. Saunders.
Engels, Friedrich
  1973   *The Condition of the Working-Class in England.*
          Moscow: Universal Publishing.
Enright, John B.
  1970   "An Introduction to Gestalt Techniques." In *Gestalt
          Therapy Now,* ed. Joen Fagan and Irma Lee Sheperd,
          pp. 107–124. New York: Harper Colophon Books.
Ewen, Stuart
  1976   *Captains of Consciousness: Advertising and the
          Roots of the Consumer Culture.* New York: McGraw
          Hill.
Eyer, Joseph
  1979   "Reply to Dr. Cooper." *International Journal of
          Health Services* 9: 161–168.
  1977   "Prosperity as a Cause of Death." *International Jour-
          nal of Health Services* 7: 125–150.
  1975   "Hypertension as a Disease of Modern Society." *In-
          ternational Journal of Health Services* 5: 539–558.
Eyer, Joseph, and Sterling, Peter
  1977   "Stress Related Mortality and Social Organization."
          The Review of Radical Political Economics 9
          (Spring): 1–44.

Fanon, Franz
  1963   *The Wretched of the Earth.* New York: Grove Press.
Feuerstein, Michael, and Skjei, Eric
  1979   *Mastering Pain.* New York: Bantam.
Fisher, Seymour
  1975   "Effects of Messages Reported to Be out of Awareness
          upon the Body Boundary." *The Journal of Nervous
          and Mental Disease* 161: 90–99.
  1973   *Body Consciousness: You Are What You Feel.* Engle-
          wood Cliffs, N.J.: Prentice–Hall.
  1970   *Body Experience in Fantasy and Behavior.* New York:
          Appleton-Century-Crofts.
Fisher, Seymour, and Cleveland, Sidney E.
  1968   *Body Image and Personality.* 2nd ed. New York:
          Dover.
Foss, Daniel
  1972   *Freak Culture.* New York: E. P. Dutton.
Foucault, Michel
  1977   *Discipline and Punish.* New York: Pantheon.
Frankenhauser, Marianne, and Gardell, Bertil
  1976   "Underload and Overload in Working Life: Outline of
          a Multidisciplinary Approach." *Journal of Human
          Stress* 2 (Sept.): 35–46.
Freud, Sigmund
  1961   *Civilization and Its Discontents.* New York: W. W.
          Norton.
Friedman, Meyer, and Rosenman, Ray H.
  1974   *Type A Behavior and Your Heart.* New York: Fawcett
          Crest.
Friedmann, Georges
  1961   *The Anatomy of Work.* New York: The Free Press of
          Glencoe.
Friedson, Eliot
  1971   *Profession of Medicine.* New York: Dodd Mead.
Fromm, Erich
  1965   *Escape from Freedom.* New York: Avon Books.
Funkenstein, Daniel H., King, S. H., and Drolette, M. E.
  1957   *Mastery of Stress.* Cambridge, Mass.: Harvard Uni-
          versity Press.

Garfinkel, Harold
  1967   *Studies in Ethnomethodology.* Englewood Cliffs, N.J.:
         Prentice-Hall.
Garson, Barbara
  1981   "The Electronic Sweatshop." *Mother Jones* 6 (July):
         32–41.
  1977   *All the Livelong Day.* New York: Penguin.
Gellhorn, Eric
  1969   "The Consequences of the Suppression of Overt
         Movements in Emotional Stress: A Neurophysio-
         logical Interpretation." *Confinia Neurologica* 31:
         289–299.
"Genetic Tests by Industry Questions Rights of Workers"
         New York Times, Feb. 3, 1980: 1.
Gioscia, Victor J.
  1967   "Adolescence, Addiction and Achrony." In *Personal-
         ity and Social Life,* ed. Robert Endelman, pp. 330–
         345. New York: Random House.
Glass, David
  1977   "Stress Behavior Patterns and Coronary Disease."
         American Scientist 65 (Mar.–April): 177–187.
Glenn, Evelyn Nakano, and Feldberg, Roslyn L.
  1977   "Degraded and Deskilled: The Proletarianization of
         Clerical Work." *Social Problems* 25 (Oct.): 52–64.
Goffman, Erving
  1974   *Frame Analysis.* New York: Harper and Row.
  1961   *Asylums.* Garden City, N.Y.: Doubleday-Anchor.
  1959   *The Presentation of Self in Everyday Life.* Garden
         City, N.Y.: Doubleday-Anchor.
Goldberg, Herb
  1976   *The Hazards of Being Male: Surviving the Myth of
         Masculine Privilege.* New York: New American
         Library.
Gordon, James S.
  1980   "The Paradigm of Holistic Medicine." In *Health for
         the Whole Person,* ed. Arthur Hastings, James Fadi-
         man and James Gordon, pp. 3–27. Boulder, Colo.:
         Westview Press.

Gore, Susan
  1978   "The Effect of Social Support in Moderating the
          Health Consequences of Unemployment." *Journal of
          Health and Social Behavior* 19: 157–165.
Gracey, Harry L.
  1972   *Curriculum or Craftsmanship.* Chicago: University of
          Chicago Press.
Greenfield, Norman S., Roessler, Robert, and Crosley, Arthur P.
  1959   "Ego Strength and Length of Recovery from Infec-
          tious Mononucleosis." *Journal of Nervous and Men-
          tal Diseases* 128: 125–128.
Grossinger, Richard
  1980   *Planet Medicine.* Garden City, N.Y.: Doubleday.
Gruchow, William
  1979   "Catecholamine Activity and Infectious Disease Epi-
          sodes." *Journal of Human Stress* 5 (April): 11–17.
Gubrium, Jabor F.
  1975   *Living and Dying at Murray Manor.* New York: St.
          Martin's Press.
Guttmacher, Sally
  1979   "Whole in Body, Mind and Spirit: Holistic Health
          and the Limits of Medicine." *Hastings Center Report*
          9 (No. 2): 15–21.
Habermas, Jürgen
  1968   *Knowledge and Human Interests.* Boston: Beacon
          Press.
Haraszti, Miklos
  1978   *A Worker in a Worker's State.* New York: Universe
          Books.
Harburg, Ernest, Blakelock, Edwin H., and Roeper, Peter J.
  1979   "Resentful and Reflective Coping with Arbitrary
          Authority and Blood Pressure." *Psychosomatic Medi-
          cine* 41 (May): 189–202.
Harburg, Ernest T. Erfurt, Haunstein, L., Chape, C., Schull, W.,
and Shork, M.
  1973   "Socio-ecological Stress, Suppressed Hostility, Skin
          Color and Black-White Male Blood Pressure:
          Detroit." *Psychosomatic Medicine* 35: 276.

Hauser, Stuart T.
    1981   "Physician-Patient Relationships." In *Social Contexts of Health, Illness and Patient Care*, ed. Elliot G. Mishler et al., pp. 104–140. New York: Cambridge University Press.
Heim, Edgar, Knapp, Peter H., Vachon, Louis, Globus, Gordon G., and Nemetz, Joseph S.
    1968   "Emotion, Breathing and Speech." *Journal of Psychosomatic Research* 12: 261–274.
Henig, Robin M.
    1981   *The Myth of Senility.* Garden City, N.Y.: Doubleday-Anchor Press.
    1978   "Exposing the Myth of Senility." *The New York Times Magazine* (Dec.): 159–167.
Henley, Nancy M.
    1977   *Body Politics.* Englewood Cliffs, N.J.: Prentice-Hall.
Holmes, Thomas H.
    1980   "Stress: The New Etiology." In *Health for the Whole Person*, ed. Arthur Hastings, James Fadiman and James Gordon, pp. 345–356. Boulder, Colo.: Westview Press.
Holmes, Thomas H., and Rahe, Richard H.
    1967   "The Social Readjustment Rating Scale." *Journal of Psychosomatic Research* 11: 213–218.
Holub, William R.
    1979   "Holism in Nutrition." *Journal of the Nutritional Academy* 11 (Oct.): 38–42.
House, James S., McMichael, Anthony J., Wells, James A., Kaplan, Berton H., and Landerman, Lawrence R.
    1979   "Occupational Stress and Health among Factory Workers." *Journal of Health and Social Behavior* 20 (June): 139–160.
House, James
    1974   "Occupational Stress and Coronary Heart Disease: A Review and Theoretical Integration." *Journal of Health and Social Behavior* 15: 17–27.
Ichheiser, Gustav
    1970   *Appearances and Realities.* San Francisco: Jossey-Bass.

Illich, Ivan, Zola, Irving Kenneth, McKnight, John, Caplan,
Jonathan, and Shaiken, Harley
    1977   *Disabling Professions*. London: Marion Boyars.
Ingber, Dina
    1981   "Brain Breathing." *Science Digest* 89 (June): 72–75.
"Is Holistic Political?"
            The San Francisco Bay Guardian, July 4, 1979: 3, 9.
Jahoda, Marie
    1958   *Current Concepts of Positive Mental Health*. New
            York: Basic Books.
Janowitz, Morris
    1975   "Sociological Theory and Social Control." *American
            Journal of Sociology* 81: 82–108.
Jennings, Charles, and Tager, Mark J.
    1981   "Corporate Wellness Programs: Good Health Is Good
            Business." *Medical Self Care* no. 13 (Summer): 14–18.
Johnson, Allen
    1978   "In Search of the Affluent Society." *Human Nature* 1
            (Sept.): 50–59.
Johnson, James H., and Sarason, Irwin G.
    1978   "Life Stress, Depression and Anxiety: Internal-
            External Control as a Moderator Variable." *Journal of
            Psychosomatic Research* 22: 205–208.
Jourard, Sidney M.
    1964   *The Transparent Self*. New York: D. Van Nostrand.
Kagan, Aubrey, and Levi, Lennart
    1974   "Health and Environment: Psychosocial Stimuli: A
            Review." *Social Science and Medicine* 8: 225–241.
Kahn, Robert L.
    1981   *Work and Health*. New York: Wiley.
Kass, Leon R.
    1975   "Regarding the End of Medicine and the Pursuit of
            Health." *Public Interest* 40 (Summer): 11–42.
Kastenbaum, Robert
    1971   "Getting There ahead of Time." *Psychology Today* 5:
            52–54, 82–84.
Kelleman, Stanley
    1981   "A Somatic Image of Wholeness." *The Journal of
            Biological Experience: Studies in the Life of the Body*
            3 (Mar.): 3–14.

Kingsport Study Group
    1978   "Smells Like Money." *Southern Exposure* 6
             (Summer): 59–65.
Kiritz, Stewart, and Moos, Rudolf H.
    1974   "Physiological Effects of Social Environments."
             Psychosomatic Medicine 36 (Mar.–April): 96–114.
Kleinman, Arthur
    1978   "The Failure of Western Medicine." *Human Nature* 1
             (Nov.): 63–68.
Kohn, Melvin L.
    1969   *Class and Conformity: A Study in Values.* Home-
             wood, Ill.: The Dorsey Press.
Koos, Earl L.
    1954   *The Health of Regionville.* New York: Columbia
             University Press.
Kuhn, Thomas S.
    1970   *The Structure of Scientific Revolutions.* 2nd ed.
             Chicago: University of Chicago Press.
Laing, R. D.
    1979   *Self and Others.* Baltimore, Md.: Penguin.
Laing, R. D., and Esterson, A.
    1965   *Sanity, Madness and the Family.* New York: Basic
             Books.
Lakoff, Robin
    1975   *Language and Woman's Place.* New York: Harper and
             Row.
Larkin, Ralph
    1979   *Suburban Youth in Cultural Crisis.* New York:
             Oxford University Press.
Lasch, Christopher
    1979   *The Culture of Narcissism.* New York: W. W.
             Norton.
Lauer, Robert H.
    1973   "The Social Readjustment Scale and Anxiety: A
             Cross-Cultural Study." *Journal of Psychosomatic
             Research* 17: 171–174.
Lazarus, Richard
    1966   *Psychological Stress and the Coping Process.* New
             York: McGraw-Hill.

Lefcourt, Harold M.
1973   "The Function of the Illusions of Control and Free-
        dom." *American Psychologist* 28: 417–425.
Lerner, Michael
1979   "Surplus Powerlessness." *Social Policy* 9 (Jan.–Feb.):
        1–10.
Lessing, Jill
1981   "Denial and Disability." *Off Our Backs* (Special Issue
        on Women and Disability) 11 (May): 21.
Levi, Lennart
1981   *Preventing Work Stress.* Reading, Mass.: Addison-
        Wesley.
1978   "Quality of the Working Environment: Protection
        and Promotion of Occupational Mental Health."
        Working Life in Sweden, no. 8 (Nov.).
Liem, Ramsay
1981   "Economic Change and Unemployment: Context of
        Illness." In *Social Contexts of Health, Illness, and
        Patient Care*, ed. Elliot G. Mishler et al., pp. 54–78.
        New York: Cambridge University Press.
Luce, Gay Gaer
1971   *Biological Rhythms in Human and Animal Physiol-
        ogy.* New York: Dover.
Lynch, James J.
1979   *The Broken Heart.* New York: Basic Books.
MacGregor, Frances Cooke
1974   *Transformation and Identity.* New York: Quadrangle.
Mann, Edward W.
1973   *Orgone, Reich and Eros.* New York: Simon and
        Schuster.
Marcuse, Herbert
1955   *Eros and Civilization.* Boston: Beacon Press.
Marx, Karl
1977   *Capital, Volume One*, trans. Ben Fowkes. New York:
        Vintage.
1964   *The Economic and Philosophic Manuscripts of 1844*,
        trans. Martin Milligan. New York: International.
McKeown, Thomas
1979   *The Role of Medicine.* Princeton, N.J.: Princeton
        University Press.

Mechanic, David
    1978A   *Medical Sociology*. 2nd ed. New York: Free Press.
    1978B   *Students under Stress*. Madison, Wisc.: University of
             Wisconsin Press.
Melzack, Ronald
    1974   *The Puzzle of Pain*. New York: Basic Books.
Merton, Robert
    1968   *Social Theory and Social Structure*. New York: The
            Free Press.
Mills, C. Wright
    1956   *White Collar*. New York: Oxford University Press.
Monat, Alan, and Lazarus, Richard S., eds.
    1977   *Stress and Coping*. New York: Columbia University
            Press.
Moore, Wilbert E., and Tumin, M.
    1949   "Some Social Functions of Ignorance." *American
            Sociological Review* 14: 787–795.
Moss, Gordon Ervin
    1973   *Illness, Immunity and Social Interaction*. New York:
            Wiley.
Mumford, Lewis
    1970   *The Conduct of Life*. New York: Harcourt Brace
            Jovanovich.
    1962   *Technics and Civilization*. New York: Harcourt Brace
            and World.
Nathanson, Contance A.
    1975   "Illness and the Feminine Role: A Theoretical
            Review." *Social Science and Medicine* 9: 57–62.
Navarro, Vicente
    1976   *Medicine under Capitalism*. New York: Neale Wat-
            son Academic Publications.
Nichols, David C., and Tursky, Bernard
    1967   "Body Image, Anxiety and Tolerance for Ex-
            perimental Pain." *Psychosomatic Medicine* 29:
            103–110.
Nisbet, Robert
    1966   *The Sociological Tradition*. New York: Basic Books.
Nixon, Peter G. F.
    1979   "Homeostasis and Hypertension." *Journal of Psycho-
            somatic Research* 23: 423–430.

Obers, Don
  1979   "Tayloring Social Services." *Win* 25 (Aug.): 2–14.
O'Donnel, Mary
  1978   "Lesbian Health Care: Issues and Literature." *Science for the People* 10 (May/June): 18–19.
Ollman, Bertell
  1979   *Social and Sexual Revolution.* Boston: South End Press.
  1976   *Alienation.* 2nd ed. Cambridge, England: Cambridge University Press.
Panides, Wallace C., and Ziller, Robert C.
  1981   "The Self-Perception of Children with Asthma and Asthma/Enuresis." *Journal of Psychosomatic Research* 25: 51–56.
Pearlin, Leonard I., and Schoeder, Carm
  1978   "The Structure of Coping." *Journal of Health and Social Behavior* 19 (Mar.): 2–21.
Pelletier, Kenneth
  1977   *Mind as Healer, Mind as Slayer.* New York: Dell.
Pfeffer, Richard M.
  1979   *Working for Capitalism.* New York: Columbia University Press.
Piller, Charles
  1981   "Staying Healthy at Work." *Medical Self Care,* no. 13 (Summer): 6–13.
Pollard, Sidney
  1963   "Factory Discipline in the Industrial Revolution." *The Economic History Review,* 16, 2nd ser., no. 2: 254–271.
Powles, John
  1973   "On the Limitations of Modern Medicine." *Science, Medicine and Man* 1: 1–30.
Pratt, Lois
  1976   *Family Structure and Effective Health Behavior.* Boston: Houghton Mifflin.
Rabkin, Edward S., and Silberman, E. M.
  1979   "Passing Gas." *Human Nature* 2: 30–39.
Rahe, Richard, and Ransom, Arthur J.
  1968   "Life Change Patterns surrounding Illness Experience." *Journal of Psychosomatic Research* 11: 341–345.

Robinson, Paul A.
    1969   *The Freudian Left*. New York: Harper and Row.
Schmale, Arthur H.
    1972   "Giving Up as a Final Common Pathway to Changes
            in Health." In *Advances in Psychosomatic Medicine*,
            Vol. 8, ed. Z. I. Lipowski, pp. 20–40. Basel, Switzer-
            land: S. Karger.
Schmale, Arthur H., and Iker, I. V.
    1971   "Hopelessness as a Predictor of Cervical Cancer."
            Social Science and Medicine 5: 95–100.
Schnall, Peter L., and Kern, Rochelle
    1981   "Hypertension in American Society: An Introduction
            to Historical Materialist Epidemiology." In *The
            Sociology of Health and Illness*, ed. Peter Conrad and
            Rochelle Kern. New York: St. Martin's Press.
Schneider, Michael
    1975   *Neurosis and Civilization: A Marxist-Freudian Syn-
            thesis*, trans. Michael Roloff. New York: Seabury
            Press.
Schnitger, Eileen
    1981   "News Analysis: Women's Health Centers At-
            tacked." *Plexus* 8 (June): 1.
Schwab, John J., and Harmeling, James D.
    1968   "Body Image and Medical Illness." *Psychosomatic
            Medicine* 30: 51–61.
Schwartz, Barry
    1973   "Waiting, Exchange and Power: The Distribution of
            Time in Social Systems." *American Journal of Sociol-
            ogy* 79: 841–870.
Schwartz, Gary
    1979   "The Brain as a Health Care System." In *Health
            Psychology—A Handbook*, ed. G. Stone, F. Cohen, N.
            Adler, et al., pp. 549–571. San Francisco: Jossey-Bass.
"Scorecard on Flextime"
            Psychology Today 13 (Dec. 1979): 27–31.
Scott, Rachel
    1974   *Muscle and Blood*. New York: E. P. Dutton.
Seligman, Martin E. P.
    1975   *Helplessness: On Depression, Development and
            Death*. San Francisco: W. H. Freeman.

Selye, Hans
1956   *The Stress of Life*. New York: McGraw-Hill.
Sennett, Richard, and Cobb, Jonathan
1972   *The Hidden Injuries of Class*. New York: Vintage.
Shealy, Norman C.
1976   *The Pain Game*. Millbrae, Calif.: Celestial Arts.
Shealy, Norman C., and Coulter, H. C.
1979   "Debating the Issues: Rationalism vs. Empiricism."
        Holistic Health Review 2 (Spring): 34–38.
Sheridan, Alan
1980   *Michel Foucault: The Will to Truth*. New York:
        Tavistock.
Shontz, Franklin C.
1969   *Perceptual and Cognitive Aspects of Body Experience*.
        New York: Academic Press.
Smithers, Janice A.
1977   "Institutional Dimensions of Senility." *Urban Life* 6:
        251–276.
Sobel, David
1980   "Placebo Studies Are Not Just all in Your Mind."
        New York Times, Jan.: E1.
"Some Job Situations Drive Workers to Drink"
        Alcohol, Drug Abuse, and Mental Health News 6
        (August 1980): 1.
Sontag, Susan
1978   *Illness as Metaphor*. New York: Farrar, Strauss and
        Giroux.
"Special Clinics Give Russians Places to Let Off Steam"
        San Francisco Examiner and Chronicle, July 1,
        1979: 7.
Staub, Ervin, Tursky, B., and Schwartz, G. E.
1971   "Self Control and Predictability: Their Effects on
        Reactions to Aversive Stimulation." *Journal of Perso-
        nality and Social Psychology* 18: 157–162.
Stellman, Jeanne
1977   *Women's Work, Women's Health*. New York:
        Pantheon.
Stellman, Jeanne M., and Daum, Susan M.
1971   *Work Is Dangerous to Your Health*. New York:
        Pantheon.

Stone, Laurie
   1980   "Body Politics." *The Runner* 2 (Mar.): 40–47.
Strauss, Anselm, ed.
   1975   *Chronic Illness and the Quality of Life.* St. Louis:
           C. V. Mosby.
"Study Examines Tears of Sorrow."
           New York Times, Jan. 15, 1980: C1.
Syme, Leonard S., and Berkman, Lise F.
   1976   "Social Class, Susceptibility and Sickness." *American
           Journal of Epidemiology* 104: 1–8.
Terkel, Studs
   1974   *Working.* New York: Avon.
Thompson, E. P.
   1966   *The Making of the English Working Class.* New
           York: Vintage.
Totman, Richard
   1979   *Social Causes of Illness.* New York: Pantheon.
Twaddle, Andrew C., and Hessler, Richard M.
   1977   *A Sociology of Health.* St. Louis: C. V. Mosby.
U.S., Department of Health, Education and Welfare
   1973   *Work in America.* Boston: MIT Press.
U.S., Department of Labor
   1981   "Workers on Late Shifts." *Bureau of Labor Statistics,*
           Sept., Summary 81–13.
Volicer, Beverly J.
   1978   "Hospital Stress and Patient Reports of Pain and
           Physical Status." *Journal of Human Stress* 4 (June):
           28–37.
   1977   "Cardiovascular Changes Associated with Stress dur-
           ing Hospitalization." *Journal of Psychosomatic
           Research* 22 (Nov.): 159–168.
Waitzkin, Howard B., and Stoeckle, J. D.
   1972   "The Communication of Information about Illness."
           In *Advances in Psychosomatic Medicine,* Vol. 8, ed.
           Z. J. Lipowsky, pp. 180–215. Basel, Switzerland:
           S. Karger.
Waitzkin, Howard B., and Waterman, Barbara
   1974   *The Exploitation of Illness in Capitalist Society.*
           Indianapolis: Bobbs-Merrill.

Waldron, Ingrid
   1976   "Why Do Women Live Longer than Men?" *Journal of Human Stress* 2 (Mar.): 2–13.

Weber, Max
   1958   *The Protestant Ethic and the Spirit of Capitalism.* New York: Charles Scribner's Sons.

Weil, Andrew
   1973   *The Natural Mind.* Boston: Houghton Mifflin.

Weiner, Herbert
   1977   *Psychobiology and Human Disease.* New York: Elsevier.

Weinstein, Corey
   1976   "American Medicine: Rip Off and Repression." *City Miner* 43: 8–11, 41–45.

Weiss, Jay M.
   1972   "Psychological Factors in Stress and Disease." *Scientific American* 226 (June): 104–113.

Wolff, Harold G.
   1968   *Stress and Disease.* 2nd ed. Springfield, Ill.: C. C. Thomas.

Wu, Ruth
   1973   *Behavior and Illness.* Englewood Cliffs, N.J.: Prentice-Hall.

Zola, Irving Kenneth
   1972   "Medicine as an Institution of Social Control." *The Sociological Review* 20: 487–504.

Index